BELLA AND MIRABEL

MESSAGES OF DELIGHT BETWEEN AN EARTH SPIRIT AND HER HUMAN SISTER

MARY ELLEN JACKSON

Author's Tranquility Press
ATLANTA, GEORGIA

Mary Ellen Jackson/Author's Tranquility Press
3900 N Commerce Dr. Suite 300 #1255
Atlanta, GA 30344
www.authorstranquilitypress.com

Ordering Information:
Quantity sales. Special discounts are available on quantity purchases by corporations, associations, and others. For details, contact the "Special Sales Department" at the address above.

Bella and Mirabel/Mary Ellen Jackson
Library of Congress Control Number: 2024915957
Hardback: 978-1-965463-07-9
Paperback: 978-1-963636-19-2
eBook: 978-1-963636-20-8

CONTENTS

Bella and Mirabel Introduction

It began one day in my garden in 1996. It was a balmy April morning, and I was admiring the purple irises in bloom. Then I saw her. She was a tiny, brilliant, light-being sitting on top of one of the iris flowers. I was astonished and delighted at the same time. Then she vanished. It was a fleeting moment.

Later I questioned myself. It was too early for fireflies. Was I imagining things? I questioned my sanity. Finally, after much thought, I asked not to see her again. I was afraid I would *"freak out"* and become obsessed! Instead, my skepticism and mistrust hooked me, and I dismissed the incident.

A year later this little being began to come around me and fairly often. I sensed her presence but ignored it. She persisted, and I would feel my nose being tickled (of course it was itchy, I just needed to blow it) My ears were tickled (they just needed scratching) Then I began to have small accidents—dropping things, stubbing a toe, spilling water. They were never major, but just annoying enough to get my attention. I began to question myself, what was going on? Why was I having these little accidents? Eventually I became aware that these accidents were messages to me to stop what I was doing to take a break. I began to watch and listen again. I sensed this little being around me. I began talking to her in my mind, and occasionally I would talk out loud to her in the kitchen. This was the place where I had most of the accidents and there, she could get my attention. I have a picture window at the sink, and I would stop periodically to admire the trees in blossom and the daffodils in bloom in springtime or the beautiful fall color. It was always a great refreshment for my spirit.

Out of the blue one day, I began calling her Bella. The name just came to me. She in turn calls me Mirabel. Even now she is dancing around me delighted that I am writing our story. She is not alone; she has her pals. I have been told they love to skate up and down my aura or comb it when it becomes entangled with emotional situations.

The message I received from Bella began sometime around 2000. It took me a while to write automatically, but eventually it took off. I never know when she is going to be around, beckoning me to write. She is quirky and funny. She is a *deva*, a member of the nature spirits family. She loves to "blow up" into whatever the conversation is about. One minute she is a tiny pompous professor, and the next she's an old shoe, or even a bristle brush! No matter what my mood, after one of our conversations. I always leave my writings more joyous being.

Mary Ellen/*Mirabel*

February 21, 2012

Seriousness

"Hi, Bella."

"Hi, Mirabel. Well, you have taken your time to get back with us devas."

"Yes, that's true, but I've been busy."

"Mmm, we know. But you do need your fun, and why you do deign to check in with us again?"

"Well, it's my birthday tomorrow, Bella, and I guess I wanted to talk to you."

"Well, Mirabel, we don't like to be ignored and then picked up like and old shoe when it suits you!"

"What are you doing? You're blowing up into an old shoe!"

"We want to be sure you get the message. Besides, it's nice being an old shoe."

"I thought you didn't like being treated like an old shoe."

"True, Mirabel, but this calls for an explanation."

"Now, you're blowing up into your professor mode! What are you trying to tell me, Bella?"

"Stop being so serious, Mirabel, it doesn't suit you. Do a jig or something or put on that ferocious drum music. It shakes up our psyche, we love the beat, and we dance for it!"

"Now, that's funny—you little beings dancing to drumming."

"Well, we're glad your sense of humor is returning."

"What do you mean 'returning'?"

"Well, you dumped that, too, like the old shoe. You've been far too serious lately."

"You said that already, Bella."

"Well, we just want to be sure you get our drift, man!"

"Now what are you doing? ... You've changed into a big, long-haired musician with baggy pants. You're too big, Bella. It doesn't suit you, and your pants are falling off."

"Cool it, Mirabel, everything's funky."

"You're having fun with me. ... Now you're back to your professor mode."

Mirabel, write this down."

"Your voice has changed. It's deeper."

"So it is, Mirabel, so it is. This is a serious subject: seriousness in humans."

"Okay, okay, cut out the jargon. I'm ready."

"Let us begin, then. Being serious robs you of your joy, Mirabel. Humans do not take enough time out to play, and we mean *play* not watching television or going to a movie. We mean play as children do. We see fun in all our little schemes. And we create them with fun built in. You human, however, leach out all the fun in your daily activities. And we have tweaked some of you with humorous jokes and laughter at mankind's foibles. Laughter, Mirabel, is the missing key in your lives. (You're crackling again, Mirabel.) We know you're not amused. But look at your lives, Mirabel. Where is the fun? Why do humans huff and puff themselves into soulless careers? You've bought into the—how do you call it? —the 'worldview,' or ideology (now I'm being pompous) that it is proper and correct to have a worthy career. You toil for all the goodies your world dangles before you. And you buy them, Mirabel. You all think you're a success. But are you happy? (Now, Mirabel, we hear your thoughts—we will allow you your time.) Horror, what a life! … Whoops! I see you exploding, Mirabel!"

"Well, what do you expect? Some of us have to work hard to keep body and soul together."

"Come, come, Mirabel, you know there are karmic conditions factored into this."

"Okay, I hear you—and stop tweaking my nose; it's distracting me! What I'm saying is that some people have no choice but to take any job to raise their standard of living for themselves and to have a better life for their children."

"Ah, may I interrupt you, Mirabel? What's a 'better life'? One predicated by human beings in their ivory towers of institutions?"

"Now you're doing it again … blowing up like a judge pronouncing a sentence."

"Too true, Mirabel—the concept is 'You must work hard all the days of your lives. Toil is your lot. You must buy our goods to fulfill your meager lives. We have everything you need!'"

"Stop, Bella. Now your voice sounds like a death sentence!"

"Well, it is, Mirabel. It is a living death you have all bought into."

"Well, how do you suggest we live? What's your alternative? After all, we've been 'toiling' for millennia."

"Now, now, Mirabel, you're getting angry again!"

"How agree with you that we don't take time out to play, but how can we humans do that when our workdays are long? And you've gone off on a tangent again, Bella. You started off talking about playing, but never defined it. Let's play, Bella!"

"Ah, you've got me there, Mirabel. I bow to your wishes."

"You're being sarcastic, Bella—and stop tickling my ears!"

"Mirabel, we are trying to make you laugh. Fun, Mirabel. Remember

what that is?"

"Okay, okay, I got the message!"

"Do you get it? Let's see. Suppose you are peeling potatoes. I hear you already, saying, 'Where's the fun in that?' Let's ask you, Mirabel—who are you peeling the potatoes for? Yourself, or your honey, or good friends? A change occurred in your aura when I said 'honey.' This is the one you love, is he not?"

"Yes, of course."

"But, Mirabel, what about love for yourself?"

"What are you doing, Bella? You're blowing up again."

"Good, Mirabel, I'm blowing up your fun cells! They were flat, my human friend."

"Now you're being pompous."

"Let me finish. Now, where was I? Ah, yes. Fun is love and love is fun, Mirabel. When you treat your everyday tasks as fun, they cease to be chores, duties, something to be dreaded. Look at your daily life with an attitude of mischievousness. Peel the potato a different way; talk to it. It, too, has an awareness of you."

"Oh, my, where are we off to now?"

"Yes, it does, Mirabel."

"Now you're blowing up into a big potato, Bella!"

"Yes, my golden one, I am! I think I look very handsome as a potato--lots of eyes; nice, firm brown skin, and lovely white meat inside of me! Mirabel, it is I the potato that speaks. I come to you with love and gratitude. I have grown solely to serve you. That is my lot in life. Do you like that turn of phrase, Mirabel? It is a favorite of you humans. We are tweaking you again!"

"Hmm, I know you are, but pray, do continue."

"Now, Mirabel, sulky, sulky! Well, as I said, I am now a potato. How will you cook for me? Boil me, fry me, bake me? Neat idea, isn't it? Now you have to cook a talking potato! Got you there, Mirabel!"

"Somehow we've strayed from the original subject—seriousness."

"No, we haven't. We have merely spread some delicious jam over it— love and fun! Treat everything around you as conscious living things. Talk to them, and thank them for coming to you, Mirabel. Every morsel of food, every blade of grass, every animal, every bird, every insect, everything in the universe is there for your joy and use. Today practice being with that food you prepare for your lunch. Ask it if it has a message for you."

"I think you're off your little head, Bella."

"Try it, Mirabel, try it! You know, you used to dance when you prepared your food. You would dance and sing to yourself, do you remember?"

"Yes, I do, Bella. I guess I forgot when I became so busy with the house."

"Yes, Mirabel, you did. We devas love to be around humans who have fun in their lives. We send them more fun, and more fun. It gives us pleasure, Mirabel. And I know what you're thinking—what about all the hungry people in the world? How can they have fun? We will leave that for another day, Mirabel."

"You're turning into a big somber judge again, Bella. Why?"

"Well, your energy changed into a shade of gray when you mentioned hunger in the world, Mirabel. You know as well as I do that there are circumstances that must be lived out on your earth plane that we cannot interfere with. You are not part of that scene anymore. Now it is your time for fun; that is why we are here. We are the avatars of fun, and fun we mean to have with you, Mirabel! You're ready for it! Go and talk to your potatoes, Mirabel! We are off to the garden to have fun with the plants and the other flying creatures. Adios, Mirabel. We'll tickle your nose occasionally to see how you are doing!"

Message: Look at the life you have created for yourself. Is it one determined by institutions and the marketplace? Are you shackled to a job that robs you of your joy? Insert fun into your daily tasks. When you do, you will be tuned in, and seriousness will be softened.

Baking a Cake

"Good morning, Mirabel."

"Good morning, Bella. Long time no see!"

"Well, I would say that lies with you, Mirabel."

"Bella, I've thought of you constantly these last few weeks. So, it was up to you to come in and say hi. And what is this about baking a cake? I wasn't sure I heard that."

"We sneaked it in, but you were distracted."

"Hmm. Are we taking up baking lessons now?"

"Funny, funny, Mirabel. No, we are not learning how to bake cakes. That is just a euphemism. We have been listening to your conversations with your students, and we thought it was time you explained a few little things with baking a cake in mind."

"So, you've been eavesdropping?"

"Well, you can call it that if you like. Periodically we keep track of your thinking processes, Mirabel. We like to prick your armor occasionally to check if you are really grounded on this beautiful earth."

"What does baking cakes have to do with it?"

"Be patient, Mirabel, we will get there."

"I guess you will. ... What are you doing? You're blowing up into this rotund chef, complete with a white apron and tall hat. Your hat is too big, Bella. It's out of proportion to the rest of you!"

"Ah, yes, Mirabel, it is too tall for me. But you see, I am getting a point across to you."

"What point? I'm puzzled. How can a chef's tall white hat get a point across?"

"Mirabel, think, think. What does the tall hat tell you?"

"A person of importance? Is it his badge of honor? Is it his trade? We know he is a chef or a cook by his hat."

"He could also be a witch in a white hat! Ha-ha, got you there, Mirabel! But you are right. It tells you something about the wearer. Are you such a person, Mirabel—all-knowing, wearing your huge hat of knowledge?"

"Now what are you doing. Bella? You're growing into a huge white hat. You look ridiculous, and now there are several of you. Come back to the subject, please!"

"Just having fun with you, Mirabel. Keep your shirt on! Let us look at your thought processes about new adventures. So, in baking a cake you gather all the ingredients first; is that not so?"

"True."

"Well, Mirabel, once you have gathered the necessary ingredients, you then proceed to mix the first ingredients together, then you add the next ingredient and so on until you have a complete better ready for baking. Hopefully you have set your oven to the appropriate temperature for this cake."

"And what has this to do with explanations to my students? I think we've gone off course again—your favorite pastime!"

"All good in time, Mirabel. If you think about the cake and its ingredients before the end product, what does that bring to mind?

"Mmm, let me think a moment. You start at the beginning. First, I see myself gathering the ingredients and putting them in order on the kitchen counter. Then I check the instructions for what ingredients to mix first, and once the mixing is done, I check to see if the oven is ready. I put the cake mix in a baking pan, then in the oven, and I set the timer. Then I allow the oven to do its work."

"Exactly, Mirabel. Now translate that into your method for teaching your students. You have been throwing information at them *ad lib*, and some of them are confused. You have not prepared the basic foundation for that information to be given."

"How do you mean, Bella?"

"Think about it, Mirabel, think about it! Realize you have a ready mix of students, all from different backgrounds, different age groups. Some are on their spiritual path, others are just beginning, and others are curiosity seekers. You approach this group with a mixture of intuitiveness and knowledge. Anytime a question is asked, check the energy of the questioner. Is it open, flat, high, closed, rigid, or tired? This is important, because as you zone in on their energy in answering the question, you are seeking to assess their knowledge at this time, and also trying to tell if they will understand the answer. But you also have to remember your other participants in the class. Will the answer be understandable to them as well?"

"I'm confused, Bella. How does this relate to ingredients in a cake?"

The ingredients, Mirabel, are every experience, every pothole you have ever fallen into, every book you have read, every teacher you have met, and every workshop you have attended on your spiritual journey. Which ingredients do you take out of your pantry for this group? Begin at the beginning, Mirabel. What were your first steps? Keep it simple. If you go into too much detail in your teaching, confusion will reign!"

"Now what are you doing, Bella? ... You've blown up into a miniature fat king with a wobbly crown on your head."

"Just getting a point across, Mirabel. Your guidance is knowledge mixed with intuitiveness. How grand is that!"

"You're being facetious ... and quit blowing up like a balloon! I see you've returned to your chef's guise. How about giving me an example, Bella? ... Now you're messing around again, playing a drumbeat on pots and pans. And that hat of yours is wobbling—it's about to fall off into your cake batter!"

"Okay, Mirabel, we just wanted to make sure you're not getting too serious. We can hear your brain cells firing up—and there's smoke coming out of your ears!"

"Funny, funny. Get on with it, Bella."

"As I was saying, Mirabel, knowledge mixed with intuitiveness."

"Bella, what are you doing now? ... You're blowing up into a bespectacled professor. You're distracting me!"

"Exactly, Mirabel. Stay cool, man!"

"Oh, I give up. Just get on with it. I'm getting impatient!"

"Keep your shirt on, Mirabel. Here's an example: say someone asks you the difference between working with the heart and mind or working from the intuitive side of the mind. To keep the answer simple, Mirabel, think of yourself when you struggled to understand this three-pronged question. Go into your inner wisdom and pull out of your box of goodies one that is appropriate for the level of the questioner in his or her spiritual path. In other words, the questioner may be at the very beginning and have so much conflicting information in his head already that it is important you answer one step at a time—that is, address the question from the left side, the logical mind, and then from the right side, the intuitive mind. Most humans are left-sided thinkers only. When the intuitive side kicks in, there is a gut reaction, and you feel 'That's it! That's the answer!' You have felt this many times, Mirabel. But now let us look at the heart. It requires practice to live from the heart, Mirabel."

"Don't remind me, Bella. Even now I sometimes wonder if I'm working from my heart or have slipped back into my logical mind."

"Yes, Mirabel. Your questioner is pondering the same dilemma. *Feelings*, Mirabel, *feelings. Your heart feels*. The logical mind has a set of programs all lined up, and most humans answer according to one of those programs. The heart, on the other hand, sits still, quietly waiting for you to ask it what it thinks or feels. (It thinks too; I just had to slip that in!) But its mode of thinking is done with love, generosity, compassion, and all the virtues that make up the compassionate being that you are, Mirabel."

"Thank you, Bella. Now you've touched my heart. It feels joy. I'm grateful to you for that."

"Yes, Mirabel, the heart feels joy; it longs to play its part in the spiritual journey. When the heart is asked for assistance, it will talk to your Higher Self and the soul. The intuitive mind is then filled with sparks of insight, and the logical mind strings together the details."

"Mmm, food for thought, Bella."

"Yes, Mirabel, food for thought. The cake is baked! You have your ingredients, then the mixing, and the baking, all three—the heart, the intuitive mind, and the logical mind!"

"Very noble, Bella! See you around."

"You too, Mirabel. I'm off to a well-earned party with lots of cake! This is too much like work for me!"

Message: When guiding others, it is important to take into account their spiritual maturity and mental comprehension of the subject. Like the cake metaphor, make sure to get the correct information ready, and then express it with clarity and compassion.

The Challenge

"Good morning, Mirabel."

"Good morning, Bella. I knew you were flying around me, you, and your pals, but I wasn't sure you were going to come up with anything to write."

"Ah-ha, yes, I did, Mirabel. You will be surprised at this one. We know you have written about challenges before. But today we will discuss a different version."

"Okay, this should prove interesting."

"Challenges—how do you earthlings perceive them? Be patient with me while I get into my pompous self."

"Oh, heck, here we go."

"Some of you perceive challenges as hurdles, adventures, and mistakes, while still others of you perceive them as learning experiences. Whichever type of challenge is accepted, the earthling will give it its attention. For all of you, the challenge, whether it is perceived as a hurdle, adventure, mistake, or learning experience, is a growth experience set up for you by your soul. When the earthling is ready for a major leap in its evolution, the soul hands it to you on a platter. It is still your choice whether to accept this gift or not."

"*Gift*, Bella? I can think of many challenges and experiences that I and others could have well done without!"

"Let me finish, Mirabel, as another journey unfolds before you. You do set up these situations long before you come onto the earth plane. You know that."

"Yes, you're right, but I sometimes wonder why we set up some certain experiences."

"You know that too, Mirabel."

"What are you doing? … I see you charging down a long avenue waving your arms and skipping."

"Yes, Mirabel, we are having some fun here. We don't want you to fall into your seriousness mode."

"Mmm, yes, I see what you mean. But I can't keep up with you when you're running so fast. Slow down, please."

"Is this slow enough for you, Mirabel?"

"Yes, but now you're swelling up into a big balloon! And you're waddling on two tiny feet! You look grotesque, Bella!"

"Good, I have your attention now."

"Get on with it, Bella. You know I am a busy lady today, with too much to do."

"That's it, Mirabel, the challenge!"

"What is? What are you talking about?"

"Your challenge today is to stay focused in the present moment, because you have a challenging day ahead of you. As you said, you have a lot to do. However, what's important is not what you have to do but how you approach your day, particularly those little challenges you have set up for yourself. For you, Mirabel, the real challenge is to hang loose and not lose your cool or become overly anxious because you think you will not get everything done. Do you get my drift, Mirabel?"

"I think so. What you are referring to is my tendency to become overwhelmed by all the details of a project, right?"

"Yes, Mirabel, you are correct. Your past has a tendency to loom over you like some huge gray cloud. For quite some time you had been working on healing old programs. Your previous thinking had been one of anxiety and disturbed sleep anytime you took on a new challenge. You have healed this old program and walk in confidence with a new belief that you can do anything within the limits of your physical being. You are ready to fly, Mirabel."

"You're going off on a tangent again, Bella."

"Yes, oh, golden one, I am. Sometimes it is necessary to remind you of your past successes, especially in areas of which you had no conscious knowledge. Are you with me so far, Mirabel?"

"Yes, I am. What you are saying is that in the past I became anxious and nervous anytime I ventured into a new growth area."

"Yes, that is so. Now you are off on another challenge, but it is an exciting journey for you. However, it is the details that have a tendency to derail you, Mirabel."

"Too true, Bella. Details, details are the bane of my life."

"Well, let us see what we can unravel for you. Why are details the bane of your life, Mirabel?"

"I'm not sure; otherwise, they wouldn't faze me. ... What are you doing, Bella? Oh, no, you're unraveling skeins of wool. Bella, you have dozens of them!"

"Just trying to make a point, Mirabel. The details are rather like unraveling wool. This is fun!"

"Oh, no, this is too much! What a mess you've made, Bella!"

"Just watch, Mirabel, be patient."

"That's all I can do."

"Now, where were we? ... Ah, yes—the answer to your dilemma lies deep within you, Mirabel. You just haven't taken the time to question your reaction to details. What happens when you think about all the little details of a task?"

"Mmm, this is a tough one, Bella."

"No, it isn't, Mirabel, you just don't want to face it."

"Yes, that's part of it, but not all. I think part of it has to do with time. I find that time runs away from me when I'm attending to details, especially when I could be doing something more worthwhile."

"That's it! That's it, Mirabel!"

"What is? What are you inferring? ... And now you're blowing up into a stern schoolmarm brandishing a stick! Stop, Bella! Where are we going with this?"

"Listen to what you said—that word— 'worthwhile'! That is an insight into the details challenge, Mirabel. You think and feel that all details are not worthy of your time. So, what happens? When the thought of details jumps into your mind, before you know it you are befuddled and confused, not sure which one to tackle first."

"Yes, you're right. The details become a confused bunch of energy in my mind. I feel them now as I think of my day ahead."

"Okay, let's unwind the mess!"

"Thanks, Bella, you're being facetious now. And you're back to unraveling wool. What is the purpose?"

"Patience, Mirabel. What is happening in your body as we do this? We didn't discuss feelings when we brought up details. So, what is happening in your stomach?"

"Originally it tightened up, but now it's beginning to relax. As you unravel the wool, my stomach and diaphragm relax. I breathe deeply, too."

"That is good, Mirabel. You're now beginning to relax at a deep level. This is your first task when dealing with details: become relaxed by using breathing exercises. It helps calm the mind. Now that you are becoming calmer and more relaxed, even your typing is slowing down, and you don't make as many mistakes. Now, where were we? Ah, yes, the unraveling. You do this at a physical level by writing down in order what you want to accomplish that day. Then you mark off the most important items to be undertaken. Again, a deep breath. What will you complete on this list? Slowing down, Mirabel, puts you right in the flow. Feel that flow. Stay with it for a moment. You are exactly at a pivotal point when the mind begins to relax into a deep meditation and yet remains alert enough that it can record what we are saying to you."

"This is a worthy journey, Mirabel. It is one giant leap into total relaxation in all of your daily busyness. You will feel this peace anytime you stop for a minute and breathe deeply. It also offsets any intruding anxiety that energy forms. Breathing deeply will put you in the flow again. Go to your daily details today, Mirabel, with trust. We will tweak you if we see you are slipping into a befuddled state."

"Thank you, Bella. I do feel very relaxed—almost too much so!"

"Ah, that is because you do not trust that you will achieve all your little goals today with lightness of heart. Practice this and feel the results, Mirabel. I'm off to your garden. Adios, Mirabel."

"Adios, Bella."

Message: Challenges can be daunting especially if they require in-depth research involving many details. Breathe deeply when you become fazed by this and know that all details are worthy of your time and effort. When you do this, everything will fall in line.

Compassion

"With all due respect, Mirabel, you are tizzy."

"No, I'm not. I'm just a wee bit uneasy."

"Ah, ha, ha, you are in a tizzy. Come on, admit it!"

"No, I'm not admitting it. I'm just a wee bit pushed."

"Well, that's a wee bit closer to the truth. Good morning, Mirabel. My, my, you are running around this morning!"

"Okay, okay, I got your message. You don't have to yell at me. Yes, I'm a bit pushed. You would be, too, if you had all these details to attend to."

"Now, now, Mirabel. You know perfectly well that the tizziness began a week ago. I like that new word, 'tizziness.' It's got pizzazz to it! It's like a bee buzzing!"

"Have you quite finished, Bella?"

"Just having fun, Mirabel. You are certainly in a state this morning. Now, let's see, where were we? Mmm, you were feeling pressured to catch up with your home tasks, and then you were feeling lonely for contact with your little friend."

"Get off my nose, Bella, and good morning to you! I begrudgingly admit I was missing you, yet I sensed you and your pals around me in the kitchen and the garden last week."

"Yes, we were there, Mirabel. You see, you were becoming rushed and too serious and too into your students' dramas. Yes, I know you are empathic, but do you have to go overboard? After all, they have their own guides. I think we will have to begin stripping you of that 'too caring' attitude, Mirabel. You really are working too hard. Let those other good souls take on the responsibility of caring for themselves. *You did it.*"

"Yes, you're right, Bella. I did it and I went on some tough journeys of my soul. However, I do care, Bella. That's what I'm about— caring. Caring means that souls on their journeys on the earth plane are guided on their paths and then gently led back to them when they become sidetracked. You know what that's like, right?"

"Yes, I do, Mirabel. This is time for you to sit back and allow these good souls their journeys to wisdom and freedom. With that in mind, we will begin our discourse on allowing others their experiences. All souls are in their 'stuff,' as you call it, for a good reason—namely, to learn from them. So, Mirabel, be easy on yourself. You are not expected to save these good souls, only to guide them. And this guidance will kick in when they are prepared to finish up the grand experiences, they have created for themselves. Until then, Mirabel, it's hands off!"

"Boy, you're in a bossy mood this morning, Bella. All good and fine, but how can I practice my craft if I am hand-strapped? Surely, I can impart my wisdom to them, can't I?"

"Yes, you can impart your wisdom, Mirabel, but when is it the right time and not the right time to impart your wisdom? You know from your past experiences in dealing with souls who were resistant that they turned on you in anger. Is this not so, and why would this be, Mirabel?"

"Yes, I do remember those incidences in the past and often wondered why it occurred. In hindsight, I realize they were not ready to give up their little dramas. They were obviously being nourished somehow by them, or so they thought."

"Yes, Mirabel, they were being 'nourished' by them. They create a persona through which to live for a while, to gain experiences. However, the nourishment consisted of junk thoughts, much like your junk food. Feeding off these junk thoughts set up unsavory emotions, which in turn became high dramas giving the creator a delusional feeling of power. They fed themselves with this junk until they became tired of the game of self- deceit."

"Bella, why create such pseudo personas in the first place?"

"Mirabel, you must remember that all human life on the earth plane is about experiences. And the only way you learn about the polarity of the earth's plane is through experiences of a not so enhancing nature. With all due respect, Mirabel, it is *you* who have now created this overextended caring for your students. Why do you think you created this experience, Mirabel?"

"Yes, I forgot about that aspect of the learning. I kept the uneasiness at bay until it began to filter through to my muscles. It is when they began to feel tight that I realized I was harboring an energy vibration that was calling my attention for healing."

"Precisely, Mirabel. But how long did it take you to acknowledge that you had pressure building up in your muscles?"

"About a week, I think."

"Yes, Mirabel. Do you remember how long it was before you 'copped on' to your creations? Do you remember doing the same thing over and over again? Cast your mind back to the beginning of this journey, Mirabel. Examine a habit in your past that hampered you in your spiritual growth. Ah, one has come to mind—criticism! Think about that trait for a moment, Mirabel. In how many ways did it hamper you?"

"Bella, you're right. Criticism was one big heartache for me. It never ceased in those early days—correcting me, telling me what I was doing wasn't perfect, constantly correcting and re-correcting my college papers. Going over stuff in the house until I got it just so. It was an exhausting habit."

"Just so, Mirabel, and we all felt for you on our side. We could see the harshness of this habit pulling you to your knees. But we never gave up on you, Mirabel. We played around you and brought you an image of joy. When you were finally brought to your knees, you decided it was time to move on, and you surrendered it to your Divine Self, which soared to the Universal Being of All Light. Your prayer was answered. You began the journey of compassion for yourself. You began to understand how your self-criticism projected outward, and you magnetized like beings to you who also suffered. When you began the healing process, they, too, began their healing, unless they decided to stay in that program of the 'inner critic."

"Many books have been written on this trait, Mirabel, and many workshops have been established to heal this wounded self. Now, what began with one soul, or two souls, or three souls healing this inner critic has reached out to myriads of souls on their spiritual path, giving them hope through teaching, or guiding them to their beautiful inner-light filled spirit, that spirit we so love to play around. You now receive bouquets of joy from us, Mirabel. You have earned these bouquets. We are off to play. Be kind to yourself. See you around."

"Good-bye, Bella."

Message: Caretakers are reminded that all souls are here to walk their own journeys. Your primary purpose is to remember your own journey and to be aware that others who cross your path reflect your lessons. You are learning compassion through these interactions.

Passion

"Good morning, Mirabel. You have felt passion in your being all of your life. It is this emotion that has urged you ahead on an unknown journey time after time. You are a passionate lady!"

"Good morning, Bella. There I was thinking it was ambition all along!"

"No, oh, golden one. Passion has been the base of all your wanderings, your thirst for knowledge, your search for truth, your pursuit of freedom and justice. It has pushed you into dangerous situations because of your seeking for knowledge and justice. You have taken steps into the unknown to understand the nature of life on earth. For you, Mirabel, passion is like chocolate. You could not live without it. And now let us say a few words about this wonderful gift that all souls are endowed with."

"Bella, you astound me. I didn't know you had such eloquence!"

"Well, I think it is about time you accepted your passionate nature."

"You never have looked at it, Mirabel. You think it is some great emotion that is not easily handled once it is let loose. Yes, the tiger in you, Mirabel. You did not know that? Methinks, you have just buried it and are very well aware of it!"

"Bella, passion to me means unruly emotions taking over the personality and letting a riot of judgments or torrents of fanatical rhetoric loose on the world. Passion can be so destructive. I've seen enough passion unleashed on the world by passionate people who believe in their almighty right to tell others they are wrong. We have wars as the result of passion. Are you really sure that passion is such a great emotion?"

"Yes, my dear one. Passion is an essential ingredient of all good souls on the planet of the earth. Yes, we see passion running amok in certain nations and certain races—not all for the good, either. However, Mirabel, passion is needed to make change. It is the soup of change. You need it to initiate upheavals in your bodily systems to rid the body of waste accumulated over the years. The earth also must have passionate eruptions to shed its contaminants, contaminants that are then broken up by molecular activity in your atmosphere."

"Bella, you're giving me something to think about."

"We don't want you to think about it, Mirabel. We want you to feel the passion within you. You discovered it is a quiet, deep, slow-moving energy within you. If we can use the analogy, it is almost like a submarine deep in the ocean, moving at a regular motion in keeping with the ocean's rhythm. It is quite wonderful to behold within you, Mirabel. Never think it is an emotion to be feared. It does much good, although you might see it as harmful. Your passion, Mirabel, has been hunkered down in a vast chasm within you. You have very rarely let it loose in this lifetime—the reason being that you misused it in other lifetimes. However, in this one you have used it well, albeit not enough. Your fear of it still lingers on. In time you will become comfortable with it and use it to manifest your greatest desires. You have no need to be cautious in using it. It is in your voice, your heart, and present in all your cells. Every inch of you is walking passion."

"Bella, you surprise me. I can't really believe what you're saying. It seems preposterous!"

"No, Mirabel. Without your passionate nature you would be as lifeless as a dish rag, if I may use that term. Your passion has kept you on the steady path to self-enlightenment, to mastery of the spiritual tools that you require to evolve as a soul on the earth plane."

"Mmm, very interesting. I will think some more on this great emotion."

"Don't think, Mirabel, *feel!*"

"Okay, okay, keep your shirt on. You've behaved yourself this morning, Bella—no running off on tangents or blowing up into monstrosities."

"Yes, Mirabel, we matched your mood—the emotion of quite contemplation. But if you like, we can play some games on you."

"No, Bella, I'm quite happy, thank you."

"In that case, we will be off to the garden to play with our friends. Goodbye, Mirabel."

"Goodbye, Bella."

Message: Passion, that great motivating feeling within yourself, is too often repressed. It is your greatest gift for initiating change in yourself and on the earth. Allow it to ignite your quest for knowledge and wisdom.

Laughter

"It is I again, Mirabel, good morning to you."

"So, it is. What's on the menu for today, Bella?"

"You mortals have the expression laughter is the best medicine, and indeed it is."

"Are we having dissertation on laughter this morning, Bella?"

"Yes, oh, golden one, we are. It's time you relished this wonderful food! Yes, Mirabel; laughter is food. I see the wheels spinning in your head. But laughter is the cure-all for everything, to use another expression of you mortals. Without laughter, life would be dull, monotonous—and we can't have that! So, laughter then, is for you mortals a bright spot in your hectic days. And not enough of you indulge in this wonderful gift. True, there are some wonderful wits hanging out on planet earth who just love to make fun of you humans. Don't you agree, Mirabel?"

"Yes, I do, Bella, and yes, we don't laugh enough. This morning, I realized that when I became entangled in another person's stuff! But what in the world can you say about laughter?"

"Lots and lots, Mirabel. You love to talk about energy and how it affects your lives, whether it is the energy of a friendly puppy, or the greeting from a friend, or a scowl from a frustrated angelic being. Yes, angelic beings— they, too, have their off days. But to get back to laughter, it is an energy that bounces along like a Ping-Pong ball, touching both open hearts and closed hearts. It has no restrictions or prejudices. Even animals are touched by its bounce!"

"You're pulling my hair again, Bella ... and stop tickling my ears!"

"Just making sure, Mirabel, that you are not getting too serious about this."

"Okay, okay, I get the message."

"Good, let us continue. Laughter is a much-needed value in your earthly lives, because it softens the blows of the stressors in your daily living. Understand, Mirabel, that if you did not have this laughter in your lives, your nervous system could not survive the assault of your outrageous creations."

"What are you saying, Bella— 'assault of our outrageous creations'?"

"Ah, you forget, Mirabel, that you create your daily lives, and all those goodies and baddies are conveniently forgotten. So, laughter is a medicine— and its free too. It can uplift a soul immediately. It can bring cheer even to the poorest of creatures because it allows you mortals to forget the ego selves. In a split second you can shake with laughter, and all your cells will dance, and echoes of laughter will sound around your planet earth. Yes, Mirabel, it happens!"

"You've got to be kidding!"

"No, we are not, Mirabel, so laugh at that, oh, skeptical one! Laughter encourages you to see the foolishness of it all—the absurdities, the fallacies. Smile, Mirabel!"

"I *am* smiling, Bella."

"But not with your heart, Mirabel. When you smile with your heart, you know your world is perfect just as it is. You don't have to worry about that conference, that rude individual, or that precocious child. Laughter puts life in perspective. Would you not agree, Mirabel?"

"Mmm, maybe. It's hard to laugh when the world out there is full of hurting souls."

"Now, now, Mirabel. Those hurting souls, for all you know, are enjoying their captivity."

"I beg your pardon?"

"Just that, Mirabel. You good mortals create your own captivity when you become so serious about your entanglements, your muddles. You are captives of your wild and unruly dreams."

"What are you talking about, Bella? ... And now you've turned into a tiny bird with a cage around it, and it's yelling, 'Let me out, let me out!' What are you telling me?"

"Just making a point, Mirabel. We see a lot of you good mortals living in cages, engaged in pointless creations, plotting grandiose productions, strutting around like peacocks. You are running around putting out the fires of schemes gone awry. How senseless, Mirabel."

"Now, wait a minute, Bella, I think what you've just said is unkind. Many of these 'good mortals,' as you call them, are not aware of the cages they live in. How can you poke fun at them?"

"Precisely, Mirabel. We do poke fun, getting that energy of laughter moving to shake up the cages. The idea is to break the cages you have created. If we stretch or break one bar of your cages, we are happy and dance with glee. You see, we have succeeded in our fun."

"I think you and your friends are all weird! How can you be so unfeeling? Many of these good souls are in pain—yes, I hear you—of their own making, you say. But, Bella, is it right to laugh at them?"

"Now, now, Mirabel. You're getting, what is it you say, 'uptight'? You're becoming too serious. Remember, laughter is the best medicine. That is what we are doing, throwing laughter pebbles at you caged mortals, getting your attention. 'Stop, come out of your cages, and enjoy the fresh air, the birds. Laugh at the antics of the squirrels and breathe in life."

"I get your drift, Bella. I still think it's tough to laugh when life is in shambles around your feet."

"Oh, dear, we are very serious! I will have to do something about that! Laugh at your shambles, at your mishaps, Mirabel. It's all of your wonderful creations gone awry."

"Now you've changed again. You've become a mess of tangled black squiggles. What are you telling me, Bella?"

"Just that, Mirabel, a mess! The cage, along with its creations, has fallen apart and lies around your feet. Instead of crying, laugh—you've had enough! It's time to be carefree, to flow, to just be. Just think, tomorrow you can create another cage!"

"Thanks, Bella. I didn't need that sly remark, and I'm glad to see you're back to your tiny self again!"

"Of course, I just had fun making myself into a tiny, caged bird. It's good to get the feeling of being caged occasionally. It makes me realize how much I appreciate my freedom."

"Now you're jumping all over the place, just like a Ping-Pong ball. You *are* a Ping-Pong ball! I hope you're having fun, Bella."

"Of course, Mirabel. I'm poking fun at you. Laugh, Mirabel, laugh! Dig out all your funny jokes and laugh. Your heart will rejoice in its freedom. Adios, my golden one."

"Thank you, Bella. Adios."

Message: Laughter is good medicine, especially when you are feeling sorry for yourself because one of your great ideas has been a flop, or when you make silly mistakes.

Bella and Her Pals

"Good morning, Mirabel. It's about time you paid us a visit."

"Good morning, Bella. What's going on? I see dozens of you going up and down my aura and tripping all around it."

"Yes, Mirabel—you've forgotten our name for you, haven't you? It's been so long since we spoke together! And you have forgotten how to spell it, too."

"Yes, I humbly admit it's been too long, and, yes, I had forgotten my name! But I've been so busy writing up my workshops, how can I do everything in such a short day? And you know, now my body has not been cooperative. It wants to sleep in the afternoons."

"Ah, yes, Mirabel, your body. Why do you think we are running up and down your silver cord to the celestial spaces? And why do you think we are climbing all over your aura?"

"You tell me, Bella. It looks like your pals are sliding down my aura one minute and then pulling yourself up by cords of energy and then dancing on the ends of it, which appear to be curled up. You know, it really is strange! What is the purpose of all these shenanigans?"

"You see, there you go, thinking everything must have a purpose, Mirabel. What if I told you we had no purpose except to play in your auric field? How does that appeal to you?"

"It doesn't, Bella. I'm sure you're up to something."

"Of course, we are 'up to something'! We are playing in your auric field. And it is such fun. Watch what we create, Mirabel."

"It appears you're making lots of spirals and circles in my field, and the field is growing into a huge area of flowing spirals and circles, and you're inserting twinkling diamonds like stars among the spirals and circles. It's a ball of rotating, gyrating energy of spirals, circles, and stars. I look like an earth plane. This is making me dizzy, Bella!"

"Yes, Mirabel, it should dislodge your thinking processes and allow the intuitive process to come forward. We are clearing the way for more of the intuition to come in for your writing. You have been too busy with the logical stuff. It's time for you to play and have fun. So that is what we are doing. We are having fun with you. You are a tough cookie at times, Mirabel. Just think, we have spent this page getting you to relax and allowing us to do our thing—having our way with your aura. And we do enjoy playing with it, Mirabel. Besides, we like to plant roses in it, too."

"Oh, it's beautiful, Bella. I can see roses throughout my aura. Why roses?"

"They are your favorite flower, Mirabel, and we know it was a big decision to take out your front rose garden. But they are happy in their new home. So just come to your auric field periodically and check out the roses we have planted."

"I will, Bella, I will. ... What are you doing now? I can't figure it out."

"Don't figure it out, Mirabel. Just sit back and watch the light show!"

"Wow! You've stretched my aura way back in time, like a long golden string. I can't see the end of it, Bella. ... Now it's turned into a snake, gyrating as if to music. You've got to be kidding!"

"Just watch the show, Mirabel, and enjoy."

"Okay, I'm watching. Wow, I see a carpet of grass rolled up and moving down a hillside, and yet there is still green grass on the area left behind, and I'm in the rolled-up grass laughing like crazy, enjoying the roll down the hill. When I hit the bottom, you and your pals are there unrolling the green carpet and throwing flowers around me! ... Now you've taken me to a stream, beautifully white and sparkling in the sunlight and tumbling over little rocks and stones. We hop onto the stones, and you and your pals are holding my hands. When we reach the other side, we race up another green hill, doing cartwheels and exalting in the sun and soft breeze. Where is this place, Bella?"

"It's all in your imagination, Mirabel. Look at the wonderful storehouse of creative imagination you have locked into your aura!"

"What do you mean 'locked into my aura,' Bella?"

"Yes, Mirabel, we are pulling away shades from your spiritual eyes so that you can see more and more of who you are at a spirit level. And your aura carries the DNA of these imaginative creations. Let us show you. ... Suppose we pull on a cord over here, let us say in the middle of your back. Watch what happens, Mirabel."

"It opens a space that's filled with people, gadgets, and stuff. I'm not sure what. But they are all busy doing something. Then I see this area of my spine has energy running up and down between my mind that looks like a golden ball, but my features are visible. And the energy is sent down my spine to the middle of my back to an open doorway. Within I glimpse golden doors, but the scene fades, and I see you and all your pals sitting in a circle on curled-up edges of my aura."

"We are resting, Mirabel, resting and enjoying the fruits of our labors. We still like to tweak you about 'labor,' that horrible word!"

"My aura is like a golden disc and it's rotating in a counterclockwise motion, and you and your pals are swinging off of it. It looks like a merry- go-round! ... You are all letting go one by one and flying through the space around the disc. Finally, you land on the ground— or whatever—and giggle your tiny heads off. You and your pals really are like small children, Bella!"

"Of course, we are, Mirabel!" "Oh, dear, I've forgotten to play."

"Yes, our lovely Mirabel, you have! It's time for our play. Enough! We'll see you in the garden, golden one."

Message: Remember to allow play into your life, especially when you become too immersed in your daily activities. Sometimes you forget to relax, and your body wants to rest. When this happens, it is time to refresh yourself with playfulness.

The Bristle Brush

"Good morning, Bella."

"Good morning, Mirabel."

"My, you are flitting around this morning. You're floating like a dandelion puffball. You are a puffball! What are you up to, Bella?"

"Well, Mirabel, we plan to take you on an erudite journey with a bristle brush."

"A bristle brush?"

"Yes, Mirabel, a bristle brush."

"Now you're a bristle brush. Whatever are you talking about, Bella?"

"Now, Mirabel, calm down. We have a little scheme in mind to get your lovely golden self-up and dancing with glee."

"Good try, Bella. I do need something this morning to get me going."

"Well, Mirabel, we will do that. And you are sighing, lovely one. We can't have that. So here goes! There are bristle brushes and bristle brushes, Mirabel. We want to use two kinds of bristle brushes to teach you mortals about your trials and tribulations here. This is how you perceive your experiences—as trials and tribulations. Well, now we will show you an analogy using a hard bristle brush and a soft bristle brush. Are you with me so far, oh, golden one?"

"No, but don't let me stop you."

"Well, now, this calls for being a big puffed-up balloon as I go into my professor mode."

"Bella, you look ridiculous! And get on with it."

"All in good time Mirabel. Now where was I? Ah, yes, the hard bristle brush. You have two bristle brushes, Mirabel, is this not so?"

"Yes, but you know, I get the feeling you're going off on a tangent again."

"No, just making sure you are in the bristle brush mode. So let us continue. There was a time long ago when you used a hard bristle brush on your hair. You brushed vigorously every morning and every night.And we watched you with glee. Your lovely head of hair being stretched and pulled and every hair sighing, waiting for the ordeal to be finished."

"Ordeal, Bella?"

"Yes, Mirabel, ordeal! Can you possibly imagine what it is like for your hair cells to be subjected to such brutality?"

"Come now, Bella—brutality? You're joking, of course!"

"No, we are not, Mirabel. You subjected your beautiful hair cells to a car wash! Yes, those huge bristle brushes scrubbing your car. I think that's a good analogy."

"Honestly, Bella, what are you rambling on about? And stop flying around; you're making me dizzy!"

"You need a bit of dizziness, Mirabel; your body is taut this morning."

"Bella, would you please get back to the subject?"

"Okay, okay. We liken the hard bristle brush to your life, Mirabel. You see, you spent many years putting yourself through a rigorous discipline to bring your stubborn ego into line with goodness, kindness, compassion, and so on, and so on. What a travesty! You humans put yourselves through all of these trials, and along the way your lovely bodies are dragging their tails and sighing, 'Not another goofball journey. It's time we rebelled!"

"Wait a minute, Bella. What are you saying? 'Goofball.' How can you say that?"

"Yes, Mirabel. Now, don't get miffed. Your hair is beginning to bristle! Ha-ha! You see, Mirabel, you subjected yourself to hardship and struggle when you could have achieved the desired result with the grace of joy and softness. Instead, you pushed and shoved, and huffed and puffed, until you met your desired goal. And we sighed as we watched you doing all that hard work instead of just moving with the flow. Think of your lovely hair, Mirabel, subjected to all of that vigorous brushing. Your life was given the same treatment! 'Must do this right,' 'must discipline myself,' 'must fix this, fix that,' and so on. One long march of 'musts! You know, Mirabel, I think we will get you mortals to eliminate 'must' from your vocabulary! How much easier and relaxed your lives would be."

"May I butt in for a moment, Bella?"

"Of course, you may. We couldn't have this discourse without your input. Carry on."

"The way I see it, we are taught this. We have it hammered into our little heads as children to be on time for school, be on time for meals, say your prayers, wash your hands, don't play with your food, did you do your homework? As we grew older, the rules became tougher. There was no shirking our duty. You had to practice for hours to gain mastery on the piano. You learned discipline. And now you're saying there's another way? Come on, life has to be taken by the scruff of the neck and brought into line!"

"Exactly, Mirabel— 'taken by the scruff of the neck.' Your beautiful neck dragged along like a stubborn two-year-old who won't cooperate. No wonder it hurts at times."

"Have we gone off on a tangent again, Bella? ...And now you're a long broom sweeping up my fallen hair. What are you doing?"

"Just that, Mirabel. Except your fallen hair is the 'musts' and 'fix-its.'"

"I'm butting in again, but would you please give me an example?"

"Yes, oh, golden one! Do you remember brushing your lovely hair one morning and you stopped in midair and had that intuitive flash of insight? You had just bought yourself a new hairbrush with a softer bristle. And as you brushed your hair, you felt the gentleness of the brush, its softness against your scalp, and it pleased you. You felt nurtured, and your hair felt it too. It settled down into a comfortable snooze as you brushed with gentleness. You tried to be vigorous, but the bristles defeated you. They knew what to do, and so you let go and allowed the gentle brushing of the hair to continue. Are you with me so far, Mirabel?"

"Yes, I am. I remember that morning vividly. I was startled when I had the intuitive insight. I saw in a flash how I had tackled my spiritual journeys with determination. By golly, this trait, that habit, and that program were going to be fixed! I forged ahead like a race car driver determined to win."

"Yes, our golden one. Periodically, we would blow bubbles at you to get your attention. Sometimes it worked. Other times we had you trip over yourself in your conversation with others, and then you would laugh. How delighted we were to see your cells being recharged with laughter. You knew in that instant that you could have accepted your frailties with gentleness and cushioned your spiritual journeys with compassion."

"Are you saying that all of those experiences were for naught? I'm not feeling too good about this conversation."

"Yes, Mirabel, you are feeling a little put out. But cheer up; there is an alternative way, as you learned that fateful morning. Remember the softer bristle brush? You achieved the desired results, did you not?"

"Yes, I did, Bella. But you haven't answered my question."

"Ah, yes, Mirabel. Just a minute while I get into my professor mode."

"Bella, are you laughing at me? ... Now you've turned into a rotund professor, puffing on a pipe. And your voice has deepened. All right, Bella, I got the message. Cool it!"

"Ah, you are getting it, Mirabel? Now, let's move on. Your experiences were not for naught. They served you up to a certain point. However, you outgrew the arduous trials, but you ignored the message. You were so tuned in to hardship that you forgot to listen to your caring soul, which was vying for your attention. It kept knocking on your door, calling, 'Mirabel, stop. It doesn't have to be hard anymore. You are done!'"

"Yes, I remember equating the softer bristle brush with my life. I didn't have to work so hard after all. All I had to do was to commit myself and surrender to the universe. Oh, and listen, of course. I agree with you, Bella. My journeys are so much more flowing and harmonious these days. I am more relaxed, and my energy is functioning at a higher rate."

"You've got it, Mirabel. You are spinning at a higher rate of acceleration. I must say, we love to see your cells spinning at this rate. They emit sparks. It's cool, as you humans say! Do you think we have said enough on this topic, Mirabel?"

"I should say so, Bella, and now you can return to your normal, tiny self!"

"All's well that ends well, Mirabel. Isn't it wonderful that you don't have to be a hard bristle brush anymore? Laugh at yourself, Mirabel; your cells will love it. Adios, our golden one."

"Adios, Bella."

Message: When you are on your spiritual path, once you have done the heavy-duty spiritual work, you do not have to work so hard on future journeys. Eliminate the words "should" and "must" from your life, they set you up for driving yourself too hard. Instead, let yourself go with the flow.

Junk

"Good morning, Mirabel. My, we are in a tatty state this morning!"

"What do you mean by 'tatty,' Bella?"

"Just that, Mirabel. Your etheric field is in disarray—it's a mess!"

"Well, thanks for that cheerful greeting! How would you feel if you were awakened from a nightmare?"

"I seem to remember saying 'good morning,' didn't I? Where's your good humor this morning, Mirabel?"

"In the trash can, Bella. And good morning to you."

"Ah, yes, the trash can ... Hmm, we have something to say about your trash can, Mirabel."

"Oh, boy, here we go. What's on your devious little mind this morning, Bella?"

"Actually, its junk!"

"Wow, wait a minute—junk. We're going to have a discussion on junk?"

"Yes, oh, golden one. You may not believe it, Mirabel, but many of you humans load yourselves up with junk."

"Well, I agree with you there. I'm always cleaning out junk somewhere in the house, but somehow the space always gets filled up with junk again."

"Oh, I am not talking about house junk. We chuckle at you humans when you do a spring cleaning and five minutes later you are busy filling up the empty space with junk again. You don't even begin to understand, Mirabel, what is happening to you at a deep subconscious level."

"Here we go. I guess I'd better put on my seat belt while you philosophize on junk."

"Let me see, now. Where shall I begin? Ah, yes. 'Junk,' in your terms, Mirabel, means junk you bring into your homes, or even that little bag you carry around with you that you never let out of your sight. How much junk do you have in that right now, Mirabel?"

"Funny, funny! I don't have any, Bella."

"Well, I am not talking about your household or little bag of junk. I am talking about the 'tatty' junk you carry around in your etheric field."

"You've brought up that word again— 'tatty'! Would you get to the point? My patience is thin this morning."

"Yes, oh, golden one, your patience is thin, and your etheric coat is loaded with 'tatty' junk. Junk, I might say, from all of your nonsensical thoughts, irritable thoughts, judgmental thoughts, and so on. You do not realize it, Mirabel, but you humans load yourselves down with all sorts of balls and chains in the form of grievances, judgments, victimization, and other stuff. You look much like the character Marley in your famous Christmas Carol story!"

"Hold it, Bella. What do balls and chains and Dickens's Christmas Carol have to do with junk?"

"Patience, Mirabel. As I said, humans have loaded themselves down with junk, and this junk hangs around until you decide to get rid of it. But it's not that easy. First you have to recognize that there is junk clinging to your beautiful etheric coats. Second, you have to be willing to have an etheric spring cleaning!"

"All right, I'm getting your drift, Bella. How do you propose we go about an etheric spring cleaning?"

"Very simple, Mirabel, you just must have the intent to look at your junk thoughts. Pick anyone now, Mirabel. We will pause while you scan your etheric field. ... Ah, we see you have discovered one such piece of junk—displeasure!"

"Yes, Bella, displeasure it is at the moment. However, I see a lot of other junk thoughts attached to my etheric field."

"Now, don't go off and become a determined clean-sweep broom! That is too much work. We want you to focus on 'displeasure' for the moment."

"Okay, okay."

"Mirabel, your lovely cells are spinning giddily, trying to keep up with your irritable displeasure at your good spouse. You got snappy, and then you began to remember a previous occasion when this happened, and it compounded your displeasure. And then other, similar incidences popped up. You are a simmering pot of grievances right now, Mirabel. Is that not so, beautiful one?"

"Yes, I agree, Bella, but where is all of this leading?"

"We are leading you to a lovely, soft, nurturing room within you, Mirabel. You already feel it. Sit there awhile, golden one. Feel the soft serenity. Breathe it in."

"It's lovely, Bella, and you are dancing up and down on my aura, and some of your pals are here, too. Whatever it is you are doing, it feels wonderful!"

"We are untangling your mental processes from your emotional processes and at the same time misting the aura with a cleansing dew."

"Bella, this is lovely and refreshing, but what happened to all of that junk?"

"Ah, well, now it's lying around your feet waiting to be swept up. Once you decide to let go of your judgment and your displeasure, the cleaning crew will be in shortly to do a cleanup."

"Bella, why have you turned into a huge broom? What are you saying to me?"

"Just this, Mirabel, you need a big, clean sweep right now. We want to make sure you have no history left of displeasure or irritability. One clean sweep should do it. This is the junk you are harboring in your etheric field. And we might remind you, oh, golden one, that you attract like forms. What begins with one displeasure can build into a mountain of junk grievances by the end of the day. You humans love your tantrums—they give you a feeling of power, or so you think, until you fall into exhaustion with no positive solution. You feel aggrieved and think you deserve better treatment. I am now going to turn into a mountain of junk so that you get the message, Mirabel."

"Honestly, Bella, you look disgusting. Do I really have that much junk attached to me?"

"No, beautiful one. It is just a reminder of how junk accumulates when you humans hang on to your grievances and your victim roles. All that lovely energy gone to waste, and it dries up the energy of your beautiful physical being, Mirabel—like a dried-up riverbed! Let's pretend we are trash removers and move that mountain of trash."

"And how do you propose to do that, Bella? You've turned into a huge trash truck. Your wheels are too big for the truck!"

"Yes, they are, aren't they? It calls for big wheels! You call it the 'big guns.' Shall we bring them in, too, Mirabel?"

"No, this is already getting out of hand. You've gone off on one of your tangents. I did ask you how you propose to do this cleanup, remember?"

"Naughty, naughty—you're getting your hair cells in a bristle! Ha-ha! All right, golden one. We shall bring in the compassion brooms, the love, brooms, the cleansing brooms, and the healing brooms. They will sweep up the debris once the cleaning crew is done. The big wheels will drive in and divide the mountain of trash into four divisions. When it has completed its task, the cleaning crew will sort it out and put it into even smaller divisions. You and I will look at these clumps of junk and talk about them.

"Look at this small clump of junk here, Mirabel. Why did you collect this piece of grievance in the first place? What use is it? And that piece of displeasure—how much of that do you need? And that old memory of past mistakes, do you really need to hold on to that? All of it weighs you down. It's an eyesore, Mirabel. Is it really worth it, all this displeasure for something trivial? ... Now, don't get huffy, Mirabel, I can see your hair bristling again."

"It's more than an eyesore, and it is bogging me down. ... Bella don't go there. You're turning into a bog and everything's sinking into it. Come back—I got the message!"

"Good, that's better, Mirabel. Now we will bring in the brooming crew! Now that you have cleaned the house, as you say, Mirabel, we are ready to plant new seeds of goodwill, patience, and forgiveness. So, give up your tantrums, Mirabel."

"But sometimes I like to have a good tantrum. It shakes up the body and gets the blood moving."

"Mirabel, you can do that by turning on some lively music and dancing around your home. It brings a smile to your face. On those occasions my pals and I join you. We dance with glee, and we swing on your etheric coat, pretending it's a Maypole."

"Thank you for that, Bella. I do love to dance when things are getting rough. I guess I had better let you go. I'm hungry."

"Yes, Mirabel, you are. Your stomach cells are growling at us. I wonder what it is like to be a growling stomach cell!"

"Bella, don't you dare. I'm off. Good-bye, funny one." "Adios, Mirabel, until we talk again!"

Message: Holding on to grievances and judgments has a deleterious effect on your mental and physical well-being. Letting go of such "junk" can renew your spiritual energy.

A Carpet of Roses

"Good morning, Bella."

"Good morning, Mirabel. We have a surprise for you this morning, our golden one!"

"You do? I wonder what that could be."

"Well, beautiful one, it is your special day. See what we have for you."

"Good heavens, it's a carpet of roses—all colors and hues! They're gorgeous, Bella! Pale pink, deep pink, wine, cranberry, white, yellow, orange, red, and a deep maroon rose. I have never seen one that color."

"Ah, but it exists. Now we will take you on a journey back in time."

"What are you doing with all of those clocks?"

"We said we would take you on a journey back in time, Mirabel."

"Okay, I'm a bit nervous though."

"No need to be. This is a glorious journey, a journey you carved out for yourself many moons ago."

"Mmm, I can't imagine what this journey is about."

"Let it unfold, Mirabel. It's your journey, from the time you were ushered onto this marvelous planet you call earth. Put your seat belt on. We're taking off."

"Bella, you've turned into a spaceship! And a tiny one at that."

"Yes, it is tiny. You are in it along with us and many other tiny angelic beings. Actually, they have shrunk in size to fit into this tiny capsule you call a spaceship."

"I can feel the speed it is taking. … Now it has stopped, and I emerge. I see this tiny baby. It's me! But what on earth am I wearing? And what are all those things attached to me?"

"Well, Mirabel, you have arrived. Your clothes are long swaths of cloth designed to unfold as you grow. And it is special cloth. I know, you think you look ridiculous wrapped up like a mummy."

"Yes, that tiny little baby wrapped up in so many layers. It's a wonder the little thing can breathe! Pray, go on, I'm all agog with curiosity."

"Mirabel, we have to unravel some of the cloth and some of these things hanging off of it. You could say they were all of your secret desires, in boxes all golden in color. They each contain a treasure! Shall we open one?"

"Please do, I'm bursting with curiosity. I see you're picking up the one closest to my feet. It's dangling off one of my tiny toes. Honestly, Bella, how can a little baby carry all that stuff?"

"Simple—the boxes are ethereal. They weigh nothing unless you give them weight."

"How can I give them weight? They are in the past."

"Wait and see, Mirabel. You give them weight when you decide to open one on your journey here. Isn't that wonderful? All of those lovely surprises waiting to be discovered!"

"You know, Bella, I have a hunch I'm in for some real surprises."

"Yes, you are! So, let's look at this first golden box we have picked up. Open it up, Mirabel."

"Okay, I'm a bit reluctant, but here goes. … My gosh, Bella! I see myself as a little girl, rocking a cot with my baby sister in it. I'm terrified for fear she will fall out. But I see little beings hovering around my sister. She is safe."

"That was the beginning of one of your many unfolding journeys, Mirabel. See? We have unwrapped a piece of the swaddling cloth, too."

"I feel this child, her anxiety. Why is this a treasure? And you're dancing around my aura again, pulling on it, stretching it. Whatever is going on?"

"Well, it's a treasure because you have begun the journey of completion of an earlier gift from another lifetime. And we can see you are apprehensive about this. That's why we are pulling on your aura, stretching it out. We don't want you to get into the feelings or emotions of that little girl. We want you to step back and watch a movie unfold. If there is discomfort right now, we will ease it for you. We said it was your day, so we are gifting you, Mirabel."

"Okay, I'll step back."

"We will move forward in time, Mirabel. Do you see yourself taking your inner child in your arms and loving her, telling her it's all right, that she is taken care of? See the little beings of light around her? And the child did love those times in the garden when she listened to the bees and loved the bright yellow daffodils of spring and the scent of roses in summer. Now we will move fast-forward in time. … See the young girl, and then the teenager, tired and angry? That was another box you opened. See how as you became an adult you went back in time and healed those memories? You didn't realize at the time that you were learning compassion, forgiveness, and empathy for your fellow man. You conquered your desire for revenge. You carried the scar of that battle with you for many years of your earth life. But you gained a treasure—you were no longer a slave to those lower emotions. You earned a crown, Mirabel, of inner peace. See the crown embroidered on the cloth as we unfold it?"

"Bella, this is heavy-duty stuff! And the cloth is turning into a tapestry. I see lots of lessons, experiences, gifts embroidered into it. It's beautiful!"

"Yes, it is. And that's why we love being around you, tickling your nose and your ears when you become discouraged. We are trying to get your attention to remember the treasures you have gained, your wisdom, your compassion, your kindness. Now you can see the movie of your earth life; each golden box you opened contained another journey. Sometimes you hesitated, you were tired. And then you opened the boxes containing other kinds of gifts. You see the travels, the love of your beloved when he first came into your life, the prosperity, abundance. All of these are embroidered on your tapestry of life."

"You have stretched the tapestry out, Bella. It reaches out into infinity, but it's not completely unfolded."

"That's right, Mirabel. We have many more years of your earth life to play with you. And we want you to play more now. Enjoy the carpet of roses. Lie among them, smell their perfume, savor their beautiful colors. Gather them up in your arms. Roses bring you much joy, joy, and more joy!"

"Bella, why are your pals doing dancing on my aura? I can feel their tiny feet."

"Just having fun, Mirabel. We will be tickling your ears and your nose a lot today. This is your day. Can you see most of the boxes are opened now?"

"Yes, I can. My, my, I have achieved a lot in this lifetime. I found you."

"No, no, we found you. You had to be ready to receive us."

"Pardon me, are we being uppity?"

"No, we are just reminding you. Do you remember when I first showed myself to you?"

"Yes, I was astonished. It was spring. You were sitting on the petals of an iris flower; you were a tiny flash of multicolored light. I remember being astonished because of all the colors I saw in that brief instant. ... Golly Bella all of your pals are forming a line and dancing! You're doing jigs and reels. ... Oh, I can't keep up with you. You're making me dizzy!"

"Be dizzy, Mirabel, get up and dance. Put on some of that drum music. You know we love that. It's a celebration of you, your magnificent earth life. Hang up your work shoes today. It's time for the dancing shoes. Join us, Mirabel."

"Okay, let me finish talking to you. I'm off to get my dancing shoes. Don't disappear!"

"We'll be waiting for you, Mirabel. See you in the kitchen." "See you, Bella.

Message: It is good to step back from time to time to review what you have achieved in this lifetime. It helps with staying in balance, especially during the tough times.

Steaming Kettles

"Good morning, golden one."

"Good morning, Bella. You're going to talk about 'steaming kettles' this morning? You know by this time that I should be prepared for your topics, but I'm always surprised. My first thought is always, 'What in the world can she talk about on this subject?' And now it's steaming kettles. You're becoming more and more ludicrous!"

"No, I'm not, Mirabel. Just think of the grand journey we will go on with this topic. Great imagination will be used, wonderful flowery phrases, and so on."

"If you say so, Bella."

"I do say so, and mind your manners, Mirabel." "Now what have I done?"

"You're being skeptical again and dismissing me as if I were an idiot."

"How can you tell that? I haven't said a word."

"You don't have to, Mirabel. You're steaming skepticism from your ears.

Ha-ha, got you there!"

"All right, Bella. But would you stop skipping around and yelling ha-ha at the top of your voice. I get the message. I'll quiet my skeptical thoughts. You're like a willow-the-wisp this morning, flighty, and totally irresponsible."

"Now, now, Mirabel, we are playing a game with you. And if you think about it, you will realize that we have begun our topic, only you don't see it that way. You're too busy wanting to get on with the writing. You keep thinking about all that time you're wasting."

"Yes, Bella, I am. What do you expect?"

"A little consideration for my feelings. I'm trying my best to get you in a lighthearted mood. You're dour this morning, Mirabel, and that is why I and my little friends are dancing and pulling on your aura and sliding up and down on it. We desire you to be lighthearted, too!"

"Okay, you win, Bella. I'll go with the flow."

"That's good, Mirabel. Now we will commence our dissertation on steaming kettles." We are just getting into the mood, Mirabel. We shall begin! 'Steaming kettles' - what does a steaming kettle portray?"

"Oh, dear, you're blasting my eardrums, Bella. I'll behave. Steaming kettles ... hmm. Well, I suppose you could say a steaming kettle portrays an object with a hot vapor spray coming from its spout. And it emits a gurgling sound. I wonder where this is going."

"I heard that, Mirabel. I will ignore it. Think about a steaming kettle. Can you not see how similar it is to you good mortals when you become upset? And you did this morning. You became all steamed up over a silly little thing."

"To me it wasn't silly. I was trying to understand what my spouse was explaining to me. I didn't get it, because, as you know, I think differently from him. He's so technical, and I'm the opposite. I have to have visual explanations."

"Rightly so, Mirabel. And you must see how the steaming kettle relates to your own steamed-up self. You mortals take on a subject that you do not know anything about and then expect to be able to explain it or discuss it with your spouse or others. This morning was such an issue. You didn't let go when you realized you were getting into deep water; instead, you just kept going until you were steaming with frustration. You know how you pour cold water into a kettle, Mirabel, and then set it upon the stove to boil? This is in essence what you did to yourself this morning. That was very clever of your ego. It wanted a good hang-down fight, because it was bored with the way things were between you and your spouse.

"I see you are surprised, Mirabel. You didn't think of that, did you? The ego sneaking in and taking over your dialogue with your good spouse. That good soul's patience was stretched! My companions and I were sitting on the top of your closets watching with glee. We knew that eventually you would give up. But we also knew you would feel energized by that spat with your spouse. And you did, Mirabel, did you not?"

"Yes, I did, Bella. I was feeling bored, and that 'spat,' as you call it, got my blood flowing."

"Yes, Mirabel, it did. You see, you were frustrated because you did not feel your usual perky self. And your inner you decided to have a little fun, using your ego. Just like filling a kettle with water and boiling it, the kettle was a reflection of the inner you. The inner you began rumbling at the boredom, and it used your mind to create a situation with hot words between you and your spouse. You were steaming by the end of the conversation, Mirabel. However, you were enlivened, and your energy wasn't sluggish anymore."

"Yes, you're right, Bella. I was energized. But why go at it that way? I could have done something else. And the analogy of a steaming kettle?"

"It wasn't just you, golden one. It was also your spouse. He was feeling low too! He needed something to shake him up, and you were the catalyst. Likewise, the heat under the kettle was the catalyst to get the water boiling. It can now be used to make a nice cup of tea or coffee. Once it was steaming, it was ready for its purpose. You, too, Mirabel—once you became hot in your pursuit of righteousness, you were ready to let go, and you did. You decided the discussion was going nowhere—it was turning into a yelling match—and you realized it was over a triviality. My, my, Mirabel, you have progressed!"

"Thank you, Bella, and do I detect a note of sarcasm in your tiny voice?"

"Just a little, maybe. You mortals get so huffed and puffed up over the minutest things. It's no wonder your earth boils over at times. Just think of all the steam it has to contend with from you mortals!"

"Hmm. You've made your point, Bella. And don't you dare turn into a miniature earth puffing out steam. ... You did! Bella, you're steaming up my glasses. I can't see you. You're having fun at my expense."

"I am Mirabel. I'm having a steam bath! All of us are dancing in the steam. You can always turn off the kettle, Mirabel."

"What kettle? Where, Bella? This is ridiculous!"

"Yes, isn't it? Ah, but what fun we are having. Your hair is curling in the vapor, Mirabel. You look quite the wild thing! ...Ah, yes, you are beginning to loosen up. Your energy is not stodgy anymore. In fact, it is quite lighthearted. Ah, the steam has done wonders for you, Mirabel. You are your old lighthearted self once again. We have achieved our purpose this beautiful morning."

"Pray, what purpose was that?"

"To get your energy moving, to have it gurgle and steam its way through your body and finally get the blood vessels in your brain in gear for this little conversation between us."

"Well, you certainly did that, Bella. I'm ready for the rest of the day. Thank you, little one."

"You are welcome, golden one. We will leave you now, but we will be keeping an eye on you throughout the day. Tune into us, Mirabel. Au revoir."

"Au revoir, Bella."

Message: The analogy of a steaming kettle is a good example of what happens when you get steamed up over trivialities. It is good to let off steam occasionally, because it clears the air, especially in stagnant situations. However, if the conversation becomes more heated, it is time to let go.

Talking on too much

"Good afternoon, Mirabel!"

"Good morning, Bella! What's with the 'good afternoon'?"

"Well, Mirabel, we have been tweaking you, tickling your nose. And we might add, we have been doing that since yesterday. You have completely lost it."

"What do you mean, 'lost it'?"

"Just that, Mirabel. You have been going around in circles and circles involved with everyone else's business except your own, and now you feel bereft that everything has quieted down."

"Bella, what are you and your pals up to? You're turning into a bunch of chickens running around aimlessly. If that's meant to be me, I take umbrage at that!"

"Well, now, Mirabel, lately you have been a bit like those chickens. However, I must say you were totally aware of it and managed to collect all your little chicks and put them in a basket. Do you like that analogy, Mirabel?"

"Yes, I do, Bella. It's very comforting. The chickens have settled down into comfortable positions, and some are snoozing, and others are chirping occasionally. That is a lovely scene. But we're getting away from the purpose of your visit."

"There you go again, Mirabel, all business and seriousness! Lighten up, or we shall never get started."

"Okay, okay, I'm lightening up. Is that good enough for you?"

"Yes, that is much better, Mirabel. I feel your energy flowing again. Take some deeper breaths. Oh, it's lovely—we feel your breath like a gentle breeze. Your stomach has relaxed. I think I will get some of my friends to sit on it while I talk to you."

"All right, Bella, let's move on."

"Now, now, Mirabel, be gentle with yourself. Do you realize how much you had going on since January?"

"Yes, I do, Bella, but what has that got to do with chickens?"

"Because that is what you were doing, Mirabel—hatching chickens! I know that sounds silly to you. But just think for a moment, our golden one. These chickens hatched as the result of seeds you planted over two years ago. I know you are puzzled. You do not remember all the preparatory work you did."

"Bella, this is getting stranger and stranger by the minute. I can't make sense of it."

"Yes, you can make sense of it, Mirabel. Go into your heart, our golden one, and gently ask it what was that you desired to gain insight into. I'll give you a hint. Remember your thought forms about negativity? You made the decision to be watchful of them. But you did not realize how prone you were to them, and when you did, you cried in anguish. And we, your little friends, endeavored to bring peace to your hurting heart, but you were immersed in sorrow. We had to wait. And finally, you came back to your happy, funny self, and we chided you for being the Mother Superior, the disciplinarian, who had to learn humility. Remember her, Mirabel?"

"You know that was not a good time for me, Bella. I did hurt, but not because of my frailty. It was because I thought I was beyond all of that. I fell into the arms of the ego, who couldn't do enough of gnashing its teeth and wringing its hands! I forgot I was a human being, with all the trimmings and trappings that go with being human."

"Ah, yes, Mirabel. You thought you were beyond all the ego's snares. That is why we love to play around your aura. You are willing to pick up the pieces of your shattered holiness and begin anew! That requires great courage, Mirabel. That was a major seed journey for you. That hatched a few chickens—all the consequences of your thoughts and actions. But do not fret, Mirabel. You are so much-loved despite all your trimmings and trappings. I and my little friends would not desert you."

"Oh, Bella, you are so right. That was one seed that hatched. I thought I would never walk through it. It seemed I was surrounded on all sides with criticism and negativity. But now it has softened, and I've learned to love that side of my nature. But there are so many chickens, Bella! I can't imagine what the rest are."

"Yes, our golden one, you seeded other thought forms to hatch later, and one by one they hatched. You seeded the intention to assist that other golden one with the stringed instrument. You stood by her and supported her, even though you wanted to pull back and retreat into your inner self. You had to step out of your shell, Mirabel. You had to get into a business mode. This was not your cup of tea; we knew that."

"My gosh, you are so right, Bella. There were so many phone calls, followed up with written instructions, making sure everyone was contacted. But it was fun. You know, I felt I was achieving a purpose in doing that."

"Yes, Mirabel, you did feel a sense of achievement. But we saw other seeds being shown that took you away from your journey. The return home of good friends and a family member. The concern with your beloved spouse. Let that good soul do his own thing, Mirabel. He is ruminating on his next step. He is nourished and guided. I know you resist that because of his temerity toward you. He pulled on your energy coat to bring you back to your own special purpose, a beautiful being of light carrying a torch, shedding light on the path for those ready to walk in freedom. Ah, Mirabel, don't forget your own very special journey."

"You've given me a lot to think about, Bella."

"Now, don't go there, Mirabel—you do too much thinking at times. Give your brain a vacation. I think we will show you what to do."

"Oh, no, now what? Bella, you've let the chickens loose. And you've thrown away the basket. Bella, what are you doing?"

"Just making sure you take a brain vacation, Mirabel. You no longer need to be reminded of those chickens. Let them fly away and grow on their own now. Your task is completed. Be free, Mirabel, be free. Go out into the sunshine and enjoy the lovely spring day. You don't have to watch over these little chicks anymore. They are feathered with your goodness and love. Let them fly, our golden one. ... Ah, finally we have got you to release all of them. Now we can go outside and play. We will watch for you, Mirabel. Your garden calls to you. Just enjoy it. The birds await you, too. Adios, Mirabel."

"Good-bye, Bella.

Message: When you take on too much in your life, you become scattered and lose sight of your own journey. Make sure your life has a balance between taking on tasks and taking care of your inner spirit.

The Blues

"Mirabel, Mirabel, come back. You're sinking into a dark hole again! Mirabel, we want to play with you. How can we do that if you are sinking into dark holes? Come out and play. The sunshine is beautiful, the day is beautiful."

"Good morning, Bella. Yes, I'm sinking again. I feel overwhelmed with everything—too much to do, and it's the boring, detailed stuff I'm avoiding. Why do we mortals lay so much on ourselves, Bella?"

"You know, Mirabel, you do take on too much. We mean you. My playmates and I have been watching you this last week. We thought we could sneak in and get your attention, but your black mood was a deterrent. So now we are bringing out the big guns!"

"What do you mean, 'big guns,' Bella? And don't go there. ... Oh, now you've lined up in front of me six big, old-fashioned cannons! Really, Bella, what do you hope to accomplish with this charade?"

"We hope to blast the black mood out of you, Mirabel. It has gone on too long, and we are missing your lovely, gentle, funny energy. ... That's better. We saw we brought a tear to your eye, Mirabel. We would rather deal with your tears than a dark hole."

"Yes, I am in a dark place, Bella. If you can blast it out of me, I will be ever so grateful."

"This is going to take a lot of energy and imagination. But first we must address what it is that is bothering you. Is it spring? Or is it other stuff dampening your lightheartedness?"

"Oh, Bella, it's a myriad of things, from family to teaching, to my work, to just being in the garden when the weather is so beautiful. As you know, it was a long winter and the blues have lasted longer than usual."

"We know that Mirabel. But cheer up and get out in the sun. It is so good for you. It energizes you. And we can dance on your golden aura, Mirabel. We are going to play some Tin Pan Alley music for you!"

"Tin Pan Alley music, Bella? You're nuts. ... What are you doing? Good grief! You and your pals are lined up with drums, cans, washboards, and clappers. The din is terrible, Bella!"

"Get used to it, Mirabel, for we intend to blast that Old Man Blues out of you!"

"I guess I asked for that. Carry on, Bella. I'm just a mere mortal, so how can I stop you?"

"Now, now, Mirabel, brighten up! You just said the very words that caused you to drop into that dark hole in the first place!"

"What words? I didn't use any negative words."

"Oh, yes, you did Mirabel. Think back on the words you used when you admonished me."

"For goodness' sake, Bella, you're getting huffy on me. I can tell by your voice. I'm telling you I don't recall using any negative words. ... Thank goodness you've stopped that din."

"You know, if you are just going to be critical of us when we are trying to cheer you up, we will find someone else to play with."

"Oh, heck, Bella, I'm sorry. Proceed with telling me what I said. ... Now you're turning into a big huffy professor! I guess I'm in for it."

"Come, come, Mirabel, you know we care about you. However, let us proceed. You said the words 'mere mortal.'"

"Mere mortal, Bella? You have got to be joking! That's just an expression. And there you go, blowing up even bigger. I'll behave, Bella. Just get on with it."

"Honestly, Mirabel, smile, for goodness' sake. Your face won't crack. You're a miserable old bag this morning, but at least we have got you out of your hole. Ha-ha!"

"I don't think that's funny, Bella, calling me a 'miserable old bag.'"

"Well, what do you expect? We are putting on a show for you and you insist on crawling back into your dark hole. We'll take ourselves off to the sunshine if you won't play."

"No, no, Bella, stay. I know I'm being stubborn, but please stay. I promise to cooperate. … Are we going off on tangents again? You keep changing your size. One minute you're a puffed-up professor, the next you're a diminutive elf. Actually, I like the elf—it's cute! And it brings a smile to my face."

"Good, good, Mirabel. With all of our shenanigans, we have kept you from retreating into the dark hole. … That's better, Mirabel. You are softening up. The sadness around your heart is clearing, and we can see your inner smile. Now we will proceed."

"Thank you, Bella."

"When you used the words 'mere mortal,' you didn't think about what you were saying, Mirabel. Now, think a minute about those words. Feel the word 'mere,' Mirabel. While you are doing that, we will play some music for you."

"Okay, I'm thinking and feeling 'mere.' But the music is awful, Bella. It's groaning. Your pals sound like they're in agony!"

"Well, now, Mirabel, the music is groaning, as you say, but that is intentional. We want you to get into the groove of the word 'mere', Mirabel, how does it make you feel?"

"All right, Bella, I'm feeling. The word conveys the idea of being somehow dismissed. But somehow, it's derogatory, too. It's as if I'm cast aside as being nothing. ... Oh, that feels terrible, and the music doesn't help either!"

"Ah, at long last, Mirabel, you have touched on the feeling that is sending you into a dark hole. Relax. ... And when you add the word 'mortal' to it, it enlarges the feeling of being dismissed. Does it not, oh, golden one?"

"Yes, you are so right, Bella. I can feel the words 'mere mortal' conveying isolation, wanting in purpose. So many ideas are tumbling around in my mind about these words. I would have never thought about them if you had not come calling, Bella."

"Yes, Mirabel, when those words enter your golden self, they put a blight on you. You begin to feel useless, and you feel like you have nothing to offer anymore. After all, look how you dismissed your beautiful self. You went spiraling down into that dark place and mourned, Mirabel."

"Yes, Bella. I let the world, and its expectations, intrude on my self- worth. I got tired."

"Yes, you did, Mirabel. And that is why we want you to take time out and play. You deserve playtime. All of you mortals do. But we sigh in exasperation sometimes when you insist on getting the next thing done before you can relax. How many times have we heard that? You are guilty of this, Mirabel. Then your whole body sinks with the weight of these self- imposed demands. And the dark hole is opening, just waiting to gobble you up! ...Good, that brought a smile to your face! ...Okay, gang, let it roll! *Gobble, gobble, gobble. Mirabel is ready to be gobbled! She's ready to shake, shake, shake, rattle, rattle, rattle! Mir-a-bell is dancing, dancing, dancing! Ha-ha-ha, boodiboop di boop!*"

"Oh, my lord! What have I started? I don't believe it! What a din, but at least it has a rhythm! Bella, I get your drift. I'm out of that dark place. Thank you, thank you!"

"Okay, Mirabel, remember what you say is what you set up for yourself. When all those daily tasks become too much, sit down for a minute or two and make a little plan for yourself. Set up a play box and put in there only those tasks that are necessary and leave the rest for another time. Get into the play box, Mirabel, and play rather than become demanding of yourself. Pretend you have building blocks, Mirabel. See yourself building worthiness into each task and smiling when you have accomplished one. It will brighten your day, and we can play with your golden aura and have fun playing in the play box! We are off to dance to our Tin Pan Alley music!"

"Are you leaving, Bella? I was just beginning to enjoy myself."

"You are enjoying yourself, Mirabel. The Tin Pan Alley music has shaken out the cobwebs from your aura. Keep dancing, oh, golden one. Bye! We are off to the garden. Join us later, Mirabel!"

"Bye, Bella, and thanks again."

"You're welcome, beautiful one!"

Message: Watching the words you use when relating to yourself is important. Are they uplifting or demeaning? Make a plan for yourself when you have too much to do and take a break instead of constantly pushing yourself.

Lightheartedness

"Bella, Bella! Stop! You and your pals are all over the place. Get off my head and stop sliding across my desk. This is ridiculous!"

"Good morning, Mirabel."

"Good morning to all of you. What a racket!"

"Well, Mirabel, it is time for you to be lighthearted! You don't want to be sitting here typing all our words, do you?"

"No, I must admit, I don't, Bella. It's such a lovely day out there. I want to go out and play."

"And you shall, Mirabel, you shall."

"I hope so, Bella. Life is too short to be stuck indoors on beautiful sunny days."

"My, we are in a stew this morning. What's up, Mirabel?"

"Just feeling scattered this morning, Bella, and I suspect you have something to do with it?"

"Mmm, yes, we do, Mirabel. We wanted to get your attention. We did not want you to tie yourself up with lots and lots of editing this morning. We want you to ourselves."

"Now, Bella, that's exactly how I stray from my projects. ... I take back that word 'projects.' ... Oh, darn it! You've turned into a huge truck laden with lots of stuff! ... What are you doing, Bella? Are you trying to run me over? Cut it out. It's not funny."

"Ah, Mirabel, you are no fun this morning. I can see we have some work to do to get you to lighten up."

"Well, you have a point. I did wake up with all sorts of demands calling for my attention. But I'll gladly drop all of them if we can move on."

"Okay, okay, Mirabel, I'll be good. My pals and I will behave ourselves. We will sit quietly on our little picket fence while you huff and puff your way through that stack of projects you have set up for yourself, Mirabel."

"Bella, what's the idea? You've shoved a desk in front of me loaded with files. I can't even see over them. Honestly, it can't be that bad!"

"It's not, Mirabel? Think again, oh, golden one! We made it huge on purpose, Mirabel. We want to get your attention." "Okay, okay, you have my attention now. This looks like too much work! What's your point?"

"Just this, Mirabel—come out and play. We will show you how to play with those 'projects' of yours."

"Okay, you're the boss."

"Yes, I am, but a funny one and a lighthearted one!"

"You're right, Bella. I acquiesce to your demands."

"Not 'demands,' Mirabel— 'request' sounds so much better. Demand is what you do to yourself, Mirabel, and it pushes you along until you're pooped! I like that word. Can we poop for you, Mirabel?"

"Don't you dare, Bella! Can we move on now?"

"We will, once we know you are ready to be lighthearted about your day."

"I'm ready, boss!"

"Okay. Where shall we begin? Mmm, ah, yes. How about we look at that lovely garden of yours? Can you see yourself watering all of your plants, Mirabel?"

"I did that already this morning, Bella. What's your point?"

"We know you did the watering already. However, take a good look at yourself as you make the rounds of your garden. Just to remind you that we were all there too, but did you notice us? I don't think so, Mirabel. You were focused on getting the watering done. Oh, Mirabel, you mortals are so focused on getting the work done that you miss the fun in it!"

"You have me thinking, Bella. Where are we going with this dialogue?"

"Don't think, Mirabel. You do too much of that. And where we are going? Look at yourself as you water your garden. What are your thoughts?"

"Mmm, I see what you mean. I'm looking at myself watering the new plants and turning on the soaker system for the shrubs. It's just mundane stuff."

"Yes, Mirabel, just mundane stuff. How boring for you!"

"Are you being sarcastic, Bella? Because if you are, I'm taking off."

"No. What were you thinking as you watered your beautiful plants, Mirabel?"

"Am I really as bored as you said?"

"No, not really, Mirabel. You just forgot to talk to your plants. They nourish you. They give you so much pleasure. (You were busy thinking about other projects—there's that word again!) Why not be lighthearted. With them, sing to them, talk to them? Once in a while dance around your garden."

"Really, Bella, dance around my garden? You've got to be joking! I can just see the neighbors shaking their heads. 'Mrs. Jackson is losing her mind!'"

"It's your garden, Mirabel. If you want to dance in it, do it!"

"All right, Bella. I'm not even going to discuss that one. I notice also that the stacks of files are placed in strategic areas in my garden. What's that about?"

"Go to one, Mirabel, and open it."

"Okay, I will. ... Wow! This one I opened has sprites dancing all over it, and they're rearranging the contents. I can't see what this project is—oh, now I do. It's my garden notes. What's so special about them, Bella?"

"Well, Mirabel, look at my pals. What are they doing with your notes?"

"They're stringing the words along the page and making loops with them and dancing in and out of the loops. That's so funny, Bella. Now they're jumping through the letters!"

"Mirabel, we are being lighthearted and playing with your stuff. We will go into another file. Join us."

"I surely will, Bella. This is fun. What next? ... You've opened another file, except it has turned into a small house with your pals throwing stuff out of the windows. This is puzzling to me."

"Look at the stuff, Mirabel. What do you see?"

"I see old shoes, discarded dresses, and one of your pals has dressed themselves in a dress and is wearing a pair of the discarded shoes! She looks absurd, Bella, but she's having a ball. She's tottering around the garden. ... She's tripped over the dress and fallen down. She's giggling at herself. I'm getting the message, Bella. You've separated all the files. I'm looking at another one. It has a huge bureau in it with lots of drawers. Your pals are pulling out drawers and turning the contents out. ... Bella, I'm getting dizzy!"

"Okay, Mirabel, do you understand what you do to yourself? You set yourself up for all these 'projects' and then wonder why your energy has gone poof!"

"Ah, I comprehend, Bella. I'm rushing to get everything done, but while doing that I'm missing the joy of the moment—the joy of being present to myself and being grateful in this moment. Even now I'm very conscious of the keys of my computer. My fingers are so quick, lithe and confident of themselves. I never thought to thank them before, or indeed to pretend they are dancing on the keys. That thought makes typing so lighthearted. Ah, Bella, you have given me food for thought."

"Good, good, Mirabel. Just look at all of your projects as playthings, and they will take on a lightheartedness that will surprise you. We will be around to assist you, oh, golden one!"

"I feel very lighthearted already, Bella. Thank you!"

"Delighted to hear it, Mirabel. We will be around you today to make sure you keep your word."

"What word? What word?"

"Adios, Mirabel, play and have fun!"

"I will, I promise! Adios."

Message: Take a look at all of your tasks and think about why they drain you. When you become so busy pushing to get them done, your lightheartedness is strained, and your gratitude is diminished.

The Insect Word

"Good morning, Mirabel."

"Good morning, Bella. I knew you and your pals were vying for my attention this morning. So, you won out."

"Yes, Mirabel, we were watching you caring for your flowers, so we thought we would talk to you about these little beings of consciousness."

"Bella, you're buzzing like a bee this morning!"

"Yes, we are buzzing, Mirabel. We are imitating the bees in your garden.

And what a beautiful sunny morning it is."

"Oh, my, Bella. What have you done? I see hundreds of bees flying around my garden. What's going on? What are you saying to me?"

"Look carefully, Mirabel, they are not all bees!"

"I'm looking, Bella. Ah, I see little insects, all sorts of sizes. And I see twinkling lights—what are they?"

"Surely you recognize my pals dancing around the fireflies. Watch carefully, Mirabel. What are they doing?"

"This requires my focused attention. All I see are zillions of little bugs flying around, including your pals. What am I supposed to see?"

"Watch carefully, Mirabel. Do you see what is happening?"

"Why, I see patterns forming. Your pals are organizing the insects into patterns. Some are round balls, others are long strips, and your pals are darting in and out of the patterns. The sun catches the wings of some of the insects, and they look like sparkling tiny diamonds. Now two of your pals have made a circle. In the center I see a glistening dot, and little insects are marching around and around, spreading out like the spiral patterns I saw on ancient stones in Ireland. What are they creating, Bella? ... Oh, now they are stretching upward, like tall corn stalks. I can't see the middle anymore, Bella. All I see is this round wall of stalks. ... And now I see the marching insects coming around one side of the stalks. This is very puzzling, Bella. What am I looking at?"

"Mirabel don't go into that thinking mind of yours. Just enjoy what we are creating. Can you see my pals dancing on top of the stalks and some of them sliding down the stalks?"

"Yes, I can. But what's the purpose of this?"

"Purpose? Purpose? Why should there be a purpose, Mirabel?"

"Now you're getting impatient with me, Bella. I just asked a simple question!"

"Don't go off and get huffy on me, Mirabel. We are showing you the marvels of creation. You don't see it with your physical eyes, but it is going on all the time."

"I'm enjoying the spectacle, Bella. It's lovely. But I can hardly keep track of all the patterns your pals are forming."

"It's not us, Mirabel, it's the tiny beings of consciousness honoring you. They want you to play with them instead of swatting them when they get into your kitchen."

"Oh, dear, are you trying to make me feel bad? If so, you are succeeding. You know I always talk to them before I sweat them. They're not supposed to be in my kitchen. That's where I prepare food."

"That is true, Mirabel. You have your rules as we have ours. But for now, just enjoy what is happening before your eyes."

"I see a spectacular display of patterns shaped like leaves of a tree one minute, flower petals the next, then they are curly strips wriggling in and out of blades of grass. Some of them form waves of an ocean. They even sparkle like waves in the sun. I can't keep up, Bella. The patterns are too numerous."

"Good, good, Mirabel. We have your attention. Let us talk to you about what you are seeing."

"Oh, I was enjoying that, Bella. And what's this about having my attention?"

"Just that, Mirabel. We wanted to break you away from the usual routine of your day. And we have succeeded. Now sit back while we pontificate on the insect world and your flowers and whatever else you would like to hear."

"Sounds like I'm in for a long lecture."

"Not a lecture, Mirabel, just a little dissertation on the flowers and your insect world."

"Mmm, I wonder. Do go on. I'm all ears! ... No, don't go there, Bella"!

"Okay, okay! Now, where was I? Ah, yes, your world of flowers and insects. We watch you tending your garden, Mirabel. You have never

harmed the little beings of the earth, only when they stray. And that happens when a rebellious little one decides to do his or her own thing, and of course that is when you swat them.

"There is a master being in charge of the insect world, as we have a master, too. However, we are more elevated than the insects. Nevertheless, we revere them, Mirabel. Do you ever wonder at the good work they do in your garden, indeed for your human world?"

"Yes, Bella. I know from my readings they are necessary."

"Yes, they are. They are part of all of earth's creatures, plants, rocks, and water. But we will stay with your garden. You have noticed in spring how the birds love being in your garden. Your energy, golden one, nourishes them. They know you have kept the garden free of any substance that would harm the insect beings. These little consciousnesses are needed for food by the birds and because they are not a thinking species, although many of them create order and hierarchies in their little life spans. The very soil you walk on has millions of these tiny creatures all 'doing their thing,' as you say. Before you begin thinking, Mirabel, watch the display they are showing you."

"Bella, you've started me off thinking again. However, I'm enjoying the spectacle .... Now everything is lit up. It's not just your pals. The sun is shining on a multitude of these 'little consciousnesses,' as you call them, and they are all forming their own patterns. Some are stars, others are swirls. ... Some of them are dancing in circles, and one of your pals is dancing a reel in the middle of a circle. Bella, you've gone too far this time!"

"Well, I thought it was time you saw your garden through your spirit eyes. Look into your garden at your feet, Mirabel. What do you see?"

"Wow! I see lots of tiny tunnels with little creatures running up and down.... Bella, what are you doing? I see one of them carrying a jug of water, and the little thing is spilling it. What are you up to?"

"Having fun with you, Mirabel. We thought that was a nice gesture. Do look again into your earth. Can you see the order there?"

"Mmm, not really. I do see the tunnels. Ah, now you're showing me a slice of earth, and deeper down I see other little beings working away. Some are making tiny webs with their bodies. Others are forming catacombs. That's what it appears to be."

"Yes, Mirabel, be in awe and wonder at this magnificent world under your feet. Even farther down you will see larger tunnels for your animal world. Notice how they take care not to disturb the home-like structures of their insect companions. These animals know they are there to provide food for them. There is an understanding between your birds, insects, and animals that each provides nourishment for the other. Each contributes to the richness of the earth when it drops its physical body. They move on to greater service for the earth. There are no regrets. Each little being knows its place, its order in your great cosmos.

"I am being lofty here, Mirabel, so that you truly understand the great part these little consciousnesses play in human being survival. Yes, they are tiny and invisible to your eyes. However, they continue to nurture the earth and its inhabitants. They know their roles. Their beauty is evident all about you in the colorful flowers, the diversity of trees, the grasses, the numerous plant life. Your garden, Mirabel, is but a tiny reflection of the bigger picture. We love playing in it."

"Bella, you've given me a lot to think about. Well, I take that back. I mean you've given me a lot to enjoy and really see with my physical eyes. Thank you, Bella!"

"You are very welcome, oh, golden one. We shall leave you to play in your garden, Mirabel. We will be around, too. Adieu for now."

"Good-bye, Bella."

Message: Take time out to look at the marvels of creation under your feet; everything has a consciousness and a role to play. Your horizons are broadened when you walk with awareness and awe

Bridging the Gap

"Bella, what are you up to?"

"Good morning, Mirabel. What are we up to? Well, now, that is for you to guess and for us to play with you and have you explored! Ha-ha!"

"Oh, dear, is this going to be another one of your ludicrous explorations?"

"Now, now, Mirabel, would we do that to you? And how about a 'Good morning, Bella'?"

"Oops, good morning, Bella!"

"That's better. Well, now, as we said, Mirabel, we are going on a 'ludicrous'—as you deign to call it—exploration."

"Okay, I get your drift. I'm ready this morning. Shall we begin?"

"Cool it, Mirabel, we must get into the mode of operation first. I must line up all my pals and give them instructions."

"My, my, that's a first for me. I never knew you to do that before."

"I always do that, Mirabel, you just didn't know. My pals and I have a wee conference and decide on a plan of action."

"Mmm, very interesting."

* * * * * * * * *

"Welcome back, Mirabel, did you enjoy your little rest?"

"Funny, you were all around me, dancing. Actually, you were dancing in golden sunlight. It was lovely!"

"Good, I'm glad you enjoyed it. Now you are ready, let's go!"

"Bella, you and your pals are on skates. I'm on skates, too, but I can't skate!"

"You can now, Mirabel. Relax and enjoy the ride."

"You're right, I can skate. Wow, it's wonderful! I feel as light as a feather! Hey, you're going too fast for me! Where are we off to anyway?"

"Come on, Mirabel, we'll take you by the hands. Just relax and we will pull you along."

"Wow, this is wonderful. We're going very fast, Bella. Everything is flashing by—mountains, rivers, fields. ... Oh, no! We're heading toward a chasm!"

"Yes, Mirabel. Hang on to your coattails!"

"I'm scared, Bella. Can we slow down?"

"No, Mirabel, we're going to jump the chasm!"

"We're going to do what?"

"Relax, Mirabel, we will take you over the gap. Are you ready?" "I'm closing my eyes!"

"Don't tighten up, Mirabel. Be like a jellyfish, bobbing along in the ocean."

"A jellyfish? What next? All right, I'll try, Bella. But you'd better hang on to me."

"Ready? Here we go! Wheeee! Feel the air brushing against your face, Mirabel? Feel how light you are? Now we will dance up and down like a giant ocean wave! Mirabel, relax your muscles. Trust us. You are safe! ... I see you are speechless—that's a change. I know you are scared to death. Isn't that what you mortals say? But you are safe, Mirabel. Relax, and open your eyes. You're missing the best part of the journey!"

"I don't want to open my eyes. I'll get dirt in them!"

"Ah, you're thinking again. We'll put goggles on you, Mirabel. There, now, you can open your eyes. Your muscles are tightening up, Mirabel. Relax, you are safe."

"Bella, I'm shaking all over with fright. Don't you care?"

"Not particularly, Mirabel. I know you are safe, so open your eyes and enjoy the scenery!"

"Are we near the other side yet? Then I'll open my eyes."

"Not quite, Mirabel, we're enjoying the ride, too. We don't want to miss anything."

"Okay, okay, here goes … Oh, my, Bella, where are we? I see a huge canyon, snow-covered mountain peaks, green meadows, tall pine trees, and a beautiful blue sky."

"Good. Any minute now we will be on the other side. So, enjoy the ride! Did you like that little rhyme, Mirabel?"

"Forget the rhymes, Bella, and focus on getting me to the other side!"

"Now, now, Mirabel, relax. We said you were safe, and you are. You have just landed on the other side of the chasm. You bridged the gap!"

"Oh, it feels good to have my feet on the earth again. What was the big idea, Bella?"

We took you on a wonderful journey, Mirabel. You should be appreciative; not many mortals get a chance like that."

"All right don't get huffy, Bella. After all, I've never flown through space before."

"Yes, you have, Mirabel, but you don't remember your trips."

"Now that I have my breath back, what was all that about, Bella?"

"Do you always have to have a reason, Mirabel?"

"I'm not sure where this conversation is going, but I know you're up to something."

"Well, since you put it that way, yes, we are, all of us. However, we're going to take a break for a while and enjoy the daisies, the bees, and the dragonflies."

"The dragonflies—their wings are glistening in the sun. Oh, some of your pals are flying on their backs. Now, that's incredible!"

"Come ride with us, Mirabel!"

"I can't do that, Bella. I'm too big."

"Didn't we just take you skating and flying? What makes you think we can't get you to ride on the back of a dragonfly?"

"I'm at a loss, Bella. You have me all in a tizzy this morning. Okay, I give in. Take me for a ride—no, not the chasm again!"

"All right, Mirabel, keep your shirt on. Relax, close your eyes, and I'll wave my magic wand over you. ... There, now, you are tiny like us."

"Wow, so I am! How did you do that? No, don't tell me."

"Well, what are we waiting for? Climb aboard your chariot."

"I feel wobbly, Bella. Is the dragonfly safe? It appears so fragile. Okay, here goes ... Wow! I feel so lightheaded flying up and down and zooming in and out of tufts of grass and landing on daisy petals. Bella, I see into the whole daisy. I can sit on it. It's lovely and soft."

"Have fun, Mirabel. In a minute we will take you back to your earth plane."

"What? You mean to say I wasn't on the earth plane?"

"No, Mirabel, we took you to our world—the world of tiny creatures. Yes, we live on your earth plane, but it is a world within a world. We had to jump the chasm for you to experience it—bridging the gap, Mirabel!"

"I'm glad you brought that up. I thought we lost track of the topic you were going to discuss!"

"No, oh, golden one. We wanted you to experience complete freedom of movement, and in order to do that you had to relax and trust us."

"Mmm, what's going on in that little mind of yours?"

"I'm thinking, Mirabel, thinking. I do that sometimes."

"Well, don't think too hard. I'm wary when you do that."

"Oh, really? Well, now, let's see what we can do about that."

"Now, Bella, don't go off on one of your tangents. I would rather know what that journey was all about."

"Just a little experiment, Mirabel. You see, we watch you mortals, and sometimes we wonder if you ever take a break and ponder an easier way to do something. You all work so hard at making your world work for you."

"Well, that's true, but how would you do it? Wave your magic wand?"

"Now you're being sarcastic, Mirabel, and it doesn't suit you."

"Yes, you're right."

"Where were we? Ah, yes, bridging the gap. How shall we explain it, Mirabel? We watch you mortals digging and shoveling and planting and watering your cherished desires. You forget to sit back and use your imagination to conjure up your dreams."

"I'm not sure how to take that, Bella. Yes, we do sit back and plan."

"Ah, we are not talking about planning, Mirabel. We are talking about bridging the gap between your mind and that great storage unit called the imagination."

"Bella, you've changed into a huge storage container."

"Come in and find me, Mirabel. I'm having fun with your imagination."

"I can hardly hear you. Where are you?"

"Search for me, Mirabel, but first look around you. What do you see?"

"Now, that's interesting. I see lots of my ideas—some are shelved, others are pigeonholed, and still others are in the process of becoming. ... There you are. What are you doing with that wool?"

"Knitting an idea for you, Mirabel, an idea you haven't yet created. You're dreaming about it, so I decided to help you with it."

"Knitting an idea, Bella? You're joking!"

"No, I'm not. Look at it."

"You have my attention now. I have lots of ideas, Bella. For gosh sake, which one are you knitting? This is a goofy conversation!"

"Mirabel, what would you like most in your life right now?"

"Our vacation. I would like to be assured we are indeed on our way."

"Well, that's a big order, but we are knitting ideas about this for you. Look at the pattern, Mirabel. Remember, you have to bridge the gap between your logical mind and the imagination storage unit. That means trusting that you can do it. Take the leap, Mirabel!"

"All right, Bella, but how can I just do that? My mind wants to get busy with planning and researching and everything else."

"Mirabel, stop thinking and go into your imagination storage unit!"

"Okay, Bella, I will, I will. Wow! It's full of ideas, and your pals are. dancing all over them. And there you are, busily knitting. Let me see what it is. Mmm, I see a scarf with lots of pictures on it. It's lovely, Bella. It has a plane, a cruise ship, and a train. I see lots of people. We're taking the train up the mountains. Wow! It's gorgeous scenery. It's Alaska! Bella, I'm speechless. But how is this going to translate into earthly terms?"

"Focus on the vacation, the sunny weather, the beautiful scenery, the mountains—all that will give you pleasure. Keep the dream alive, Mirabel. Feel it. And as you do, you bridge the gap. When everything is in place in the dream, it will materialize in your time."

"Bridging the gap––it seems impossible to me. … Bella don't go there. Shoot, you've turned into a huge monster with several eyes and tentacles. You look terrifying!"

"What did you expect, Mirabel. You said that horrible word. — 'impossible'!"

"I'm sorry, but I'm being human. You win, Bella. What other words of wisdom do you have for me this morning?"

"Just this, Mirabel. You are a magnificent mortal, but you can't see it, because you are all dressed up in the paraphernalia of the earth plane, which hampers you. It also blinds you to your inner magic. Use your magic with trust and have fun with it, Mirabel. Then your earthly plans will unfold without all the hard work. Do you comprehend, oh, golden one?"

"Yes, I do, Bella. What a journey we traveled this morning!"

"Yes, Mirabel, we have our fun with you, wouldn't you say? Now we are off to have our own fun, knitting more dreams for you to unravel on the earth plane."

"Oh, lord, what am I in for? Don't tell me. It's time to end this discussion."

"Yes, it is, Mirabel. We will go and dance in the daisies and ride on the backs of the dragonflies. Au revoir, Mirabel."

"Au revoir, Bella."

Message: You can dream your dreams into reality using your vast imagination storage unit combined with your logical mind. Using the latter on its own can be stultifying to your progress.

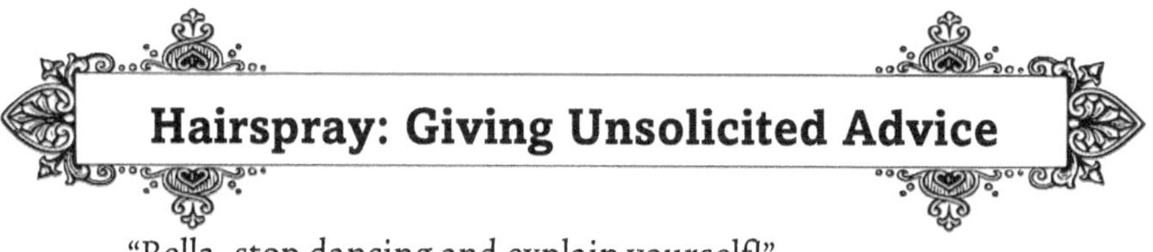

Hairspray: Giving Unsolicited Advice

"Bella, stop dancing and explain yourself!"

"Good morning, Mirabel. Just what I said—'hairspray'!"

"I don't think it's funny. And stop giggling. All your friends are laughing their little heads off, too. Are you having a laugh at my expense, Bella?"

"Now, would I do that to you, Mirabel?"

"Yes, you would. I don't trust your sense of humor at times."

"Now, Mirabel, don't get all grumpy on me. Let's begin our masterpiece."

"What choice do I have?"

"That's right, Mirabel, what choice do you have? You could close your computer and walk away, but you won't do that, Mirabel, will you?"

"No, my curiosity is too great to do that."

"That's right, Mirabel, so let us begin our very deep, deep, subject."

"Okay. I can't possibly imagine what you'll say about hairspray, except its stuff you spray on your hair to keep it in place."

"Wait and see, Mirabel. First of all, we have to get into the mood."

"Oh, dear, Bella. What are you doing? You and your friends look awful, all heads of hair standing on end. Stop, it's ghastly!"

"Just making a point, oh, golden one. Now we are ready to begin. Once upon a time there were three little bees buzzing around a beautiful garden. One day one of the bees got very curious and decided to investigate the head of a human, where it got stuck in sticky stuff you call hairspray. As our little friend endeavored to pull itself out, it became more and more entangled, and so it cried out for help from its little friends. But, alas, Mirabel, this little bee could not be helped. It had become wedged in thick strands of sticky hair. And there it expired."

"Bella, this is altogether so different from your usual stories—and sad, too. What does it mean?"

"Well, Mirabel, 'hairspray' is a wonderful word to use when getting a point across to you humans. How shall I put it? Hairspray is what you humans do to yourselves when you delve into stuff you know nothing about and then get stuck. It's quite a pattern with many of you. The only ones who appear to abstain from this game are those who are too afraid or too smart. The afraid ones run a mile from anything that is unfamiliar to them, and the smart ones stand around and check it out. They decide it's too weird and turn their noses up at it. The adventurous ones check it out and make a decision. A plan of action is mapped out, other humans are drawn in, their opinions are sought, and when our human friend is ready to proceed, he does so cautiously. After all, hairspray is sticky stuff!"

"Funny, funny, Bella, but where is this going?"

"Patience, Mirabel. The hairspray represents situations in human lives that tend to be sticky, such as quarrelsome relatives or complaining co-workers. The stickiness occurs when you would rather avoid their company, or you join their company just to be polite. In the first-case scenario humans wrap themselves in a mantle of aloofness and play hide-and-seek games, a plan that eventually unravels, causing more headaches than it was worth. In the last-case scenario, humans squash their feelings altogether and join the 'woe is me' club. Then they become enmeshed in great tales of woe. Add to that, our human friend is caught in the middle when criticism of a fellow human is voiced. Eventually the sense of being trapped overcomes our well-meaning human. Withdrawal is not an option without incurring anger or criticism from our martyr."

"That sounds familiar. I've been in that situation, and it took an inordinate amount of courage to withdraw and leave. You've become very serious, Bella."

"Well, the discussion calls for seriousness. How do you like my austere skinny mode, Mirabel?"

"Your skinny mode is most unbecoming to you!"

"Ah, that's better, Mirabel. I don't want you to lose your sense of humor. I think I look great. I can wiggle and squiggle!"

"Bella, don't go off on a tangent."

"I was having fun, Mirabel, for a moment."

"Well, fine, but let's not lose the thread of the subject."

"Okay, Mirabel, now who's being serious? Where was I? Ah, yes, you said you often find yourself in like situations. This happens when you jump into situations without surveying the field. You, and thousands more of you, can't wait to use your know-how to assist your fellow humans."

"And pray, what's wrong with that? Are you saying we should not assist our fellow humans in distress? And what are you doing? I see hundreds of little Me's running amok. This is not fair, Bella!"

"Now, Mirabel, keep your shirt on. We sometimes wonder if it is not from a sense of pride and know-it-all attitudes that you humans jump into the fray."

"All right, you have a point there, Bella. But we are human, after all, and that's part of our humanity to want to assist others in sticky situations, as you say."

"Ah, but, Mirabel, do you really want to help, or is there an underlying pompous reason? 'I have the answer to your problem; therefore, I will tell you what to do!'"

"I'm not pompous, Bella. If I decide to help someone, I sincerely hope it's from my heart."

"No, Mirabel, you are not pompous, just a little fuzzy in your thinking at times, and that's because you are already doing too much."

"Oh, dear, I like to be doing, Bella. So, if I do get fuzzy in my thinking at times, it's not because I'm too busy. I'm just a bit scattered at times."

"Precisely, Mirabel. Let us show you how you look when you become scattered."

"Oh, no, what are you doing, Bella?"

"Just showing you how you look when you are scattered."

"Oh dear, I see several little me's running around in circles and hither and thither. I can't be that bad, can I?"

"Yes, you are at times, Mirabel, and by the end of the day you are tired and cranky!"

"Bella, stop cranking up a rusty old car. If that's supposed to be me, I strenuously object!"

"Object all you like, Mirabel, but this is you at the end of one of your scattered days."

"Bella. Can we get back to the subject matter?"

"All right, Mirabel, don't get huffy on me. It's all good fun! Now, where was I? Ah, yes, a sticky situation with relatives. Mmm, the hairspray analogy is very good, Mirabel. All those heads of hair I showed you are the hairy situations you humans get yourselves into. Most of it is the result of your wanting to do a service for another or imposing your idea of what is right for another, and then you become stuck. Now you must extricate yourselves without hurting the other party. You have come full circle—the reason for delving into the situation in the first place, not wanting to hurt another if you refuse to be involved in their business. Ah, Mirabel, don't you see how tempting it is to be wanted and looked up to and sought out as a great wise one?"

"Bella, are you having fun with me?"

"No, Mirabel, just getting a point across."

"You have made your point, Bella, and I can barely see you. Where are you?"

"Over here, Mirabel, untangling the sticky mess so that you can cut loose from it. It's time that humans freed themselves from the affairs and entanglements of others."

"What do you suggest we do, Bella? Totally ignore our fellow humans in stress?"

"No, Mirabel. Stand back and survey the situation before you jump in. Your fellow humans got themselves into their sticky messes, so you must allow them the freedom to untangle their messes. Think of the fascinating stuff they will learn about themselves. And how will they ever discover their own mastery if every time they get into a sticky mess their fellow humans jump in with how-to tools to salvage their concoctions! Look at nature, Mirabel, how all life explores its territory and its capabilities."

"Bella, you're showing me a beautiful place. I see baby lions exploring water. I see little chicks jumping in the air and flapping their wings, - goodness, even trying to climb walls! I see seals exploring the ice, tentatively testing it with a flipper. Okay, Bella, I get your drift."

"Good, Mirabel. All those creatures are watched over by their mentors, but they are allowed to explore and learn for themselves. Be aware, oh golden one, that too much protection and enabling rescues can nobble the solution to sticky situations. I like that word— 'nobble.' I will now nobble off to play with my companions. Play in your garden, Mirabel. We feel your fingers itching to work with the earth. Go, oh golden one. We shall meet again in the sunlight. Au revoir, Mirabel."

"Au revoir, Bella."

Message: It is important to allow others to work on their issues without advice from you or well-meaning friends. You cannot know their life's challenges. By stepping in, you risk becoming enmeshed in yourself.

Hats

"Good morning, Bella. I know you are playing games with me. I see you and all of your pals wearing tall hats. What's the idea?"

"Good morning, Mirabel. Yes, we have been patiently waiting for you to get out of your 'blue funk'! Now you are ready to play with us, are you not?"

"No, I'm not if you're going to pick on me!"

"Oh, my, we are in a rambunctious mood. I like that word, 'rambunctious.' It's big and heavy!"

"Bella, cut it out. You have turned into a huge, overbearing sergeant major with medals dripping off of you! What are you saying to me?"

"Just that, Mirabel, you are being overly rambunctious. So, let's just cool it, shall we, Mirabel? I will behave if you will."

"Okay, I'll behave!

"Let me think a moment. We decided to talk to you about hats."

"Bella, I should be used to you by now, but a discussion on hats?"

"Ah, well, you see, Mirabel, hats are what you humans love to wear. How do I look in this hat, Mirabel? This is one of yours."

"Oh, dear, that hat looks too square and severe, Bella. It doesn't suit you either."

"Hopefully you understand why we put on this hat. Many humans wear lots and lots of hats, as we said. However, they don't see them, Mirabel. All during their busy days we watch them take off their hats and put on other hats. What do you think the hats represent, Mirabel?"

"We understand it to mean the different roles we play in our lives."

"Yes, Mirabel, you are correct. So many roles. Sometimes we get dizzy just watching you humans exchanging dozens of hats during the course of a day. It is amazing to us that many of you manage to hang on to your sanity."

"Are we that busy, Bella? ... Good grief, you're showing me several of my selves during the course of a day. Oneself is cooking, another is writing, another is gardening, another is shopping, and still another is on the computer! I never thought of myself with all of these selves, Bella. I wear different hats for different tasks too. Goodness, this is too much!"

"Well, Mirabel, we are just beginning our little discourse on hats!"

"Oh, dear, what am I in for?"

"Just tweaking you, Mirabel. We are using hats to demonstrate how you humans keep yourselves excited and creative. You love to have many experiences and challenges. And you don a hat for each experience. It's rather like having a lid on a tin. When you have finished using that tin, you put the lid back on, especially if it is a tin filled with scrumptious cookies! You don't want to overindulge."

"Are we into cookies now?"

"No, just keeping you on your toes, Mirabel. I'll continue. The hats—I said you make us dizzy when we watch you. If you think about it, Mirabel, humans are constantly on the go: exploring, creating, doing, all different kinds of activities. It is exciting if you humans are doing what you genuinely love to do. However, and it is a big 'however,' so many of you are playing roles you are not suited for."

"What do you mean, Bella?"

"As I said: many humans play roles they are not suited for. They do this to please their peers, or to honor the programs instilled in them from their childhood, or to feel important, or for notoriety, or some other reason. Are you getting the drift of my message?"

"Yes, pray, continue."

"We think, my pals and I, that some tins should be permanently closed. Humans are exhausting their energy reserves. Each role they play taxes their energy in a different way. Some roles do excite them with creativity, but others strain their nervous systems, and still others tax their physical bodies. It is quite amazing to us how the human body is so flexible, pulsing with constant animation. It is even being healed while you are straining its reserves. When humans are busy playing all their roles, there is a whole army of little helpers repairing, cleaning, and maintaining its systems. If humans could see the inner mechanism of their bodies at work, they would rethink the roles they play."

"Wow, Bella, I see the inner body of someone. It's a mass of moving parts!"

"Yes, Mirabel, look further into it. See the helpers I told you about?"

"Really, Bella, I see little men running around fixing what look like wires, tubes, and valves."

"Just having fun, Mirabel. However, if you look further and further into the cells, there you will see helper cells working very hard. Watch what happens when someone cuts a finger. See, at the cellular level the cells clustering around the cut, assisting it to heal. Did you know that the cells have a great love for all of your organs and indeed yourselves, Mirabel? Your beautiful bodies could not make it through their busy days without all this nurturing going on at the cellular level."

"Bella, you have quite shaken me up. I never thought of my body in this way."

"Don't go and become all serious, Mirabel. Laugh at your follies during your busy days. The hats will fall off when you do that. You begin to see the absurdity of it all."

"Bella, you have me quite confused. Why do we go in for all of this 'absurdity,' as you call it?"

"Well, now, Mirabel, you humans are dreaming machines. Anytime you dream of something, you already have it in mind to do it. It is in the doing that you become overly zealous. You forget that your creations take on a life of their own. You become their slaves, thus the many hats you wear."

"How can we possibly turn off the spigot of creativity once it takes on a life of its own? This is a thorny issue, Bella. ... Bella don't go there! It's just an expression we humans use in reference to sticky situations! Bella, stop! You've turned into a sticky, gluey mess with huge, bulging eyes. You look awful!"

"Calm down, Mirabel, I'm just having my fun. I thought I looked fantastic as a great, big, sticky globe. All right, I'll behave. Is that better?"

"Yes, I prefer your tiny sparkling self. But what is to be done with all of these hats we wear, Bella?"

"Try putting the lid on them, Mirabel. Lock them away and throw out the key. How many activities or goodies do you need in any one day? Pick the ones that bring you the most sense of achievement. Notice we did not say joy. Joy can be an entrapment, Mirabel."

"Why, Bella, we always look for the stuff that brings us joy. You have me confused again!"

"Joy, for you humans, Mirabel, has a footnote attached to it. If you do not have joy with all your busyness, you feel there is something missing, or you are not doing what is right for you. There are many activities that are not joyful but are necessary. You know from your own experience how details derail you. You forget the time they use up, and you haven't allowed for that in your eagerness to explore another adventure!"

"You are so right, Bella. I get so wrapped up in my adventures that I forget everything else."

"What are you going to do about it, Mirabel?"

"Oh, dear, decision time. I guess I'll have to decide which of my activities are most important to me and put the lid on the others!"

"Mirabel, we will be so happy to assist you with that. Well, done, decision time here we go!"

"Bella, you and your pals are strutting around, each one acting out my creations. ... Heavens, one of you is running around fixing, tying, wiping, and straightening. This is ridiculous."

"Well, Mirabel, why don't you put the lid on all that fixing you do. Everything doesn't have to be fixed right away."

"Thank you, Bella. How about you and your helpers jumping in and giving me a hand?"

"Ah, but we do, Mirabel. How many times during your day do we draw your attention to your lovely garden, the birds that flock to it, the tiny insect world that fascinates you. You, Mirabel, are one lovely, golden human, and we so much want you to stop and enjoy your creations. Take time out, Mirabel, and smell your roses, which give you so much joy. And don't forget all those little helpers inside of you busy repairing. They too would like to take time out and smell the roses!"

"Funny, funny. However, I admit I love my garden and the birds, and nature. You have given me much to think about, Bella!"

"Oh, dear, we are off, Mirabel, before you go into that thinking box of yours. Look for us in the garden. Adios, oh, golden one!"

"Adios, Bella. I'll pay more attention when I'm in my garden."

Message: During the course of a day, you take on many roles and wear many hats. Each hat represents an activity, and many of these activities you may have never thought about. Let go of unnecessary activities; they cause an energy drain on your body.

Trunks

"Good morning, Mirabel."

"Good morning to you, Bella. What grand scheme have you planned for me this morning, my little friend?"

"Wait and see what God sends you! Ha-ha!"

"Oh, we're up to tricks again, are we? Did I hear the word 'trunks? Of all the daftest things! However, I know you by now, so I'll keep quiet. Proceed, my little friend!"

"Indeed, we shall, Mirabel. You have been escaping to your garden, and we have enjoyed it with you. The birds have brought you much pleasure. But your greatest joy was in discovering a wild orchid. This tiny little flower astonished you because of its exquisite perfection. We would like you to enjoy this delicate plant while it is still blooming. It will soon hibernate. Your cold weather is approaching."

"I've been enjoying it very much. Every time I go by it, I stop to admire its perfection. Now, what's this about trunks?"

"Ah, let me see. What was it I was going talk to you about regarding trunks?"

"Bella!"

"I'll behave, Mirabel. Where's your sense of humor this morning?"

"Out on vacation. I am depleted of humor at the moment."

"Ah, that's the reason why we bring up trunks. Think about it for a moment, Mirabel, but not too hard. What do trunks mean to you?"

"Traveling. I had one when I immigrated to the U.S. It was filled to the brim. Trunks are also used for storing one's treasures or valued possessions. You've given me food for thought, Bella, so don't go off on a tangent."

"You're no fun this morning, Mirabel. Cheer up! We will dish up to you a trunk full of delicious foods for thought."

"Bella, watch it."

"Okay, okay, Mirabel, I'll be good. Let me think for a moment."

"Don't think too hard, Bella. ... Oh, dear, you've lined up dozens of trunks, all sizes and types. I guess I'm in for it now."

"If you are not going to have fun this morning, Mirabel, we are. We love our little big trunks. Just think, Mirabel what might be in them!"

"I'm waiting, I'm waiting."

"Keep your shirt on, Mirabel. The trunks contain all of the treasures you have gathered over the years. Let's peek into one. How about that golden one over there? It is not too big, but what treasures it holds! I'll lift the lid and you come and have a look. Tell me what you see, Mirabel."

"I see beautiful silver chains, crystal rings, pearls, gold bracelets, all sorts of jewels, and they're all sparkling with iridescence. It's as if they're not real and will disappear any minute. What does it mean, Bella?"

"Mirabel, these are all of the gifts and treasures that have come to you over your earth life years. Look at them with more awareness now. Do they not remind you of the pleasure they gave you when you first held them in your hands? The joy they brought you?"

"Yes, I remember, but I'm puzzled. What's so important about these trinkets? ... Bella, what have you done? All my beautiful things have changed—they're bleak and colorless!"

"What did you expect, Mirabel? You made a disparaging remark. You called them 'trinkets! How could you, Mirabel?"

"I'm duly rebuked, I apologize."

"Good. Now we shall proceed. We will change them back to their original beauty. Mirabel, go back in time to that feeling you had when you first picked up these lovely jewels. It was a good one, was it not? You felt a sense of joy and lightness of heart. When you wore them, you received many compliments. However, look closer into these exquisite treasures. Can you see the deeper meaning they had for you? Each little stone and the silver and gold chains were woven into the fabric of your life. You forgot their essence. They each resonated with your beautiful energy, oh, golden one. They vibrated with life when you wore them, particularly when you delighted in their exquisiteness. They sparkled and radiated their light outward. All who came in contact with you were affected by their energy. You, the wearer, Mirabel, gave of your energy through these sparkling treasures. They also bring you joy every time you admire them or handle them. Are you with me so far, Mirabel?"

"Yes, I am. I never thought about my jewelry in this way. To me they were pretty, and I do love to look at them and handle them occasionally. However, I wasn't aware of the effect they had on my energy when I wore them."

"Ah, well, Mirabel. They won't be effective if they lie in a jewelry box without sunlight."

"Okay, Bella. I feel sad that I neglected them."

"You didn't know, Mirabel, but now you do. Wear them with joy and allow their beauty to sparkle. I think we can move on to another trunk, don't you? ... How about this big one over here. It is strong and sturdy. What do you think is in this one, Mirabel?"

"I have no idea."

"Perhaps you should open it up."

"Wow! This one is full of all the marvelous travels I've made. I saw Gwen and Pat, my two traveling pals. Alas, they have passed on. Look at that battered old hat. I used to wear that in Australia. The sun was so strong there. ... And there's the hotel I worked at in the Outback. I watched the kangaroos coming up to the back of the hotel in the mornings. Too, I learned to sketch while working in the Outback. It was lonely out there, Bella. I yearned to be back in the city.

"You know, Bella, I was really free in those days. I traveled with Pat and Gwen from area to area. We all had jobs to support us. It didn't matter what the jobs were as long as they paid enough for us to sightsee and pay our rent. We made a lot of friends. ... And there I am, living in an old convent and sharing it with four other girls. ... And there's the old Grand Hotel where I first learned how to waitress. But I hankered for the U.S., and after a year in Australia I returned to it. My traveling pals moved on to other vistas. I settled down, but it was hard. The traveling bug was in my blood. Mmm ... yes, I cherished my freedom, Bella."

"Yes, you did, Mirabel. Anytime someone suggested you get married and settle down, you were aghast! You wanted no part of it. Let's look at another trunk. ... How about this treasure chest? The one tied with swaths of cream satin ribbon. It's a lovely golden brass color, too. I wonder what treasure this holds."

"Let's open it, Bella. I'm all excited now!"

"Okay, here we go."

"Bella, this trunk is sad! It has a layer of gray material on top. Why? I don't understand."

"Mirabel, lift the gray cloth and you will find the answer."

"I'm a wee bit nervous. ... Yes, I see what you're telling me. That was a lonely period in my life. I had no companions with whom to share my interests. I had nothing in common with my peers. I had traveled so much, seen so many wonderful things, met people from all walks of life, that I felt like an outsider. ... There I am, having lunch on my own. Oh, Bella, did I have to look back on this part of my life?"

"Yes, Mirabel. The foundation was being laid for your great journey. You began at this crossroads. You were at a way station, frightened and lonely. You ended an engagement with a soul whose ideals, you realized, did not match yours. You began questioning your life, Mirabel. You didn't know who you were, why you did what you did, and what your purpose was. The latter was a long way off into the future. In the meantime, you met someone who took you under her wing."

"Rosalie! Yes, Rosalie. She was wonderful. She helped me with so many things, understanding my life at that time and just being there for me. I saw her the first time we met. She asked for assistance with crossing a street. We became fast friends. She was like a mother to me. She was very wise. We talked long into many an evening. I found I could communicate with her. And it was during this period I met my husband—another good soul with a kind, compassionate heart."

"Yes, Mirabel, you left the way station and began another journey of your life. You were tremulous and excited at the same time. You were frightened of an intimate relationship. However, you knew you had 'come home' when you met your husband. At that time, you were not aware of how intuitive you were, Mirabel. But let us close this chest with one last scene."

"Rosalie … she's holding my hand. We're both sitting on her sofa, both of us are crying silently. She had just told me she wouldn't see me anymore. I knew what she meant. When we dried our tears, we talked about this and that, watched her cat on the windowsill busily performing its hygiene. I never forgot the last thing she said to me: 'Mary, always take care of yourself first. Everything will fall in place after that.' I didn't understand what she meant until many years later, Bella. She was a kind, beloved friend."

"Very well, my golden one, enjoy your memories."

"Let me sit with them for a moment, Bella."

"When you are ready, Mirabel, we shall proceed."

"I'm ready."

"Let's look into this big trunk over here, Mirabel."

"It's huge and it's growing in size! What's the idea?"

"Wait and see, Mirabel."

"Oh, dear, are you playing games with me?

"Just having a little fun. Don't you like this gorgeous trunk growing before your eyes? It's multicolored, too. And look at all of the designs carved on it."

"I'm nonplussed, Bella. Are you trying to tell me something? If so, I'm not getting it."

"Well, oh, golden one, find a ladder and we will both look into it."

"Funny, funny. All right, I'll get a ladder. … Stop tickling my nose, Bella. I don't want to fall off this thing if I sneeze!"

"Just making sure you are keeping your balance, Mirabel. After all, life is about balance, isn't it? And the ladder is a good analogy, wouldn't you say?"

"I wouldn't know. Are we going off on tangents now?"

"No, just being my mischievous self! Besides, the ladder represents your journeys on the earth so far, Mirabel."

"How?"

"Look into the trunk. 'Seek and ye shall find!'"

"Okay, I'll do your bidding, before you go off on one of your mad escapades."

"My, my, we are being grumpy, aren't we! What have you found, Mirabel?"

"Give me a moment. I want to balance myself on the top of the ladder."

"I'll join you. Let's have a peek."

"Oh, gosh, Bella. This trunk is full of journals, books, trips, the ups and downs in my marriage, losses, challenges, extraordinary experiences, and wisdom. I'm speechless!"

"This contains the memories of your exciting journey into wisdom, Mirabel. Enjoy it. You found the answers to all the questions you had in those early days of your journey here. You wove into the fabric of your life grand experiences of joy, love, and sadness. Through it all you began to know yourself. You discovered your power."

"Bella, I'm overwhelmed at the moment. Would you mind if I take a break?"

"By all means, Mirabel, go outside and play. We will join you. The sun is shining. Have lunch in your garden. We will round up the birds for you!"

"Thank you, Bella. See you in the garden!"

Now that we have had our fun in the garden, it's trunk time again. Mirabel, are you ready? Let's look at some of those magnificent journeys of yours, the feats you accomplished."

"Bella, what are you doing with all of those boxes, or are they cards, strung on a string?"

"Just having fun. Go ahead and take a card, Mirabel. See what it pictures for you."

"Okay. ... What a great trick! I have a card, and when I turn it over it has a picture of a Scottish stone circle. I am beckoned to enter it and do a ceremony. The being guiding me is an ancient priest who oversees the area. The ceremony had to do with my ancient lineage in that area. It felt very peculiar and yet at home!"

"Pick another card, Mirabel, from the middle, perhaps?"

"Mmm, let me see. ... This one look interesting. Wow! It's a picture of me attending seminars—many of them. I wanted to know so much."

"Keep going, Mirabel. Don't dwell on the memories. Pick another card."

"Bella, what are you up to now? I see you on a seesaw going up and down. How can you do that? Who is on the other end? ... I am!"

"Yes, Mirabel, you seesawed up and down in those early days of your journey. One minute you were delighted with all of your new experiences, the next you were skeptical. You walked away several times. What do you see on the card, Mirabel?"

"A joker! What in the world is a playing card doing in my trunk and what am I supposed to make of this, Bella?"

"Well, now, just think for a minute. What does a joker convey to you?"

"A trickster."

"Exactly, a trickster. How many times did you fall for the sham, Mirabel, only to find you had been tricked?"

"Don't remind me; it was painfully humiliating."

"Yes, it was, Mirabel. But each time, you picked up your tattered pride and marched on."

"I chalked it up to experience, but I smarted nevertheless."

"Ah, that's your humanness, Mirabel. But look at the gifts you earned— compassion, humility, kindness—and you laughed at the joke on you. The trickster was duly vanquished!"

"I learned to step back before jumping into anything."

"I think we are finished with trunks. It's time for us to go out and play."

"I was just getting into the swing of things, and you call it quits. That's not fair."

"Now, now, Mirabel, it's time for you to play. Your garden with all of its little beings of delight awaits you. Remember, they sparkle when you hang around them. So put on your shoes and join us. Au revoir."

"Okay, au revoir it is, Bella, until we meet again."

Message: Your life is full of "trunks" that hold treasures of successes and gifts of mastery. During periods of dissatisfaction, when you feel that your goals are not materializing, your treasures will remind you of your many accomplishments.

Thinking Big

"Good morning, Mirabel. Finally, you have noticed me. I have been flying around you, tweaking your nose, pulling your hair, and you just ignore me! Even my pals are vying for your attention!"

"Sorry, Bella. I knew you were around. I'm sure you saw all I had to do before I could sit down with you."

"Yes, Mirabel, I saw all of your 'have to' duties calling for your attention. However, if you had sat down with me first, your day would be much more fun-filled!"

"Well, you're right, and I did think about sitting down with you first, but, as you can see, the organized me wanted to get the most important business of the day cleared out. You know I always enjoy being with you. However, once we start our discussions, they can go on for a long time. So, your subject today is 'thinking big?'"

"Yes, Mirabel, we decided, me and my pals, that it was time for you to think big about all of your creations. 'Go for it'—isn't that what you humans say?"

"Yes, Bella, and ... What are you doing? You're growing huge! Your wings are trailing on the ground. Bella, you don't look exactly beautiful in that size. What's the big idea?"

"I'm getting in the mood, Mirabel. In order to do that, I have to blow up in size to get the feeling of bigness!"

"Stop strutting around like a peacock showing off its feathers. ... Oh, dear, you're now a beautiful peacock. I will say, you do look gorgeous in all of your bright blues and greens. And those black dots on your feathers are luminescent. ... Okay, let's get back on track."

"I like being a peacock. It gives me a certain superiority over all the other birds. And it's lovely to strut my feathered beauty for all to see!"

"Okay, I'll patiently wait while you do your thing."

"Wow, what a change that is. However, I'll behave, and we will get on with our big subject. Thinking big, Mirabel, is just that. You humans, with few exceptions, think too small. Your mind is caged. You rummage around in that cage finding all sorts of excuses because you can't think big—too little money, not enough time, 'it's a crazy idea,' 'it's dumb,' and so on and so on. That last word—'dumb'—is the worst of all for shooting down your dreams. Those nearest and dearest to you mean well when they tell you that you are crazy, but in order to grow big, you have to challenge the status quo, as you call it."

"Well, now, Bella, you've given me something to think about. Why would thinking big make a difference?"

"Mirabel, stop and consider for a moment. What happens when you expand your physical size in your mind? Do it! Stand as tall as an oak tree, Mirabel. ... Here, I will show you."

"Oh, no, there you go! Good heavens, I can't see your head, Bella.

You're too big, and this conversation is ridiculous!"

"No, it isn't, Mirabel. Try it and see how it feels to be huge. You can be fat, skinny, or svelte, your choice!"

"You're pulling my leg, Bella."

"No, I'm not. Try being very large and walk around in your imagination as a very large lady."

"Okay, okay, I'll do it."

"That's better. How does it feel up there in clouds, Mirabel?"

"Awesome!"

"Walk around, Mirabel, and sense this tall human. ... Well, how does it feel?"

"Sort of weird. Everything looks tiny. I feel like a giant!"

"Good! Feel that bigness in your mind. This is most important, Mirabel. For it is in the mind that so many of you humans think too small. Your imaginations are tied up in neat ribbons only to be looked at occasionally, but they are never let free for fear they will go berserk."

"Really, Bella? I don't think my imagination is tied up in neat ribbons. How can you say that?"

"I dare to, Mirabel. Your imagination is too tied up, but not as tightly as others, but you still think in small containers. Come back to your regular size, and then we will go into your imagination experiment with stretching it."

"Bella, now you're stretching out like a bulging universe. Any minute you'll explode. ... Forget that, forget what I said. Just explain to me!"

You are no fun, Mirabel. I'll just explode a little bit so that you can see what I mean, oh, golden one."

"Okay, I'll play the game. ... Now, that is beautiful! You're a small cloud of light sparkles. It's like watching a shoal of tiny fish, where they all come together and then move apart, each creating a pattern. The patterns are beautiful, Bella, but we're going off on a tangent. Where is this taking us?"

"Okay, Mirabel. I will shrink back to my size and get down to the serious business of 'thinking big.' Once again, Mirabel, humor me. Go into your mind and see yourself doing one of your daily tasks—pick anyone that appeals to you."

"My daily tasks ... mmm, yes. I'll choose the task of cleaning up odds and ends before I begin my day. That stuff, Bella, is so mindless, but it has to be done."

"Yes, Mirabel, it does. It's like oiling all the gears of a machine before you run it. You know it will perform smoothly when you do that. Think about your attitude before you begin that first task. You seem to approach it with a 'mindlessness' in mind."

"I do? I thought I was just impatient to get it over and done with."

"Yes, that's part of it, but your original mind approach is 'mindlessness.' You don't give the tasks the attention they deserve, thus all of these little tasks rebel."

"This is farcical! Little tasks rebel? What will you think of next, and don't go there!"

"Mirabel, you're a stuffed shirt this morning!"

"You are straying again Bella."

"No, Mirabel. Now that I am in the professor mode, I will deign to explain to you."

"I guess I deserved that."

"Let me see. We said that your mind approach was 'mindless.' You look upon all of these little gears for your daily routine or activities as nuisances. However, Mirabel, which is in charge—the feeling of impatience or the mindlessness of thought?"

"Yes, I agree, Bella. It's the feeling of impatience, because I think those little mundane chores are thankless, not worthy of my time."

"Yes Mirabel, you regard them as 'mundane,' but they are not. It is most important that the gears of your day are oiled and ready to move you into a smooth flow. But we have strayed from 'thinking big.' Let us now use this idea to start your day, oh, golden one. It's simple, really. Just see yourself as a huge or large human when you begin your daily tasks, and they will bow down to your bigness."

"You're joking, Bella."

"Would we do that to you, Mirabel? Come play with us. In your mind make yourself tall and expansive. ... How does it feel, oh, golden one?"

"Actually, it feels marvelous. I feel like I'm in charge of my world!"

"Good! That's what we want you to feel. Do you understand now when I said you humans have caged your minds?"

"I don't feel caged, but expansive—and free! Let me think a moment, Bella."

"Don't think too hard, Mirabel. Play with the feeling of expansiveness. See yourself, every time a constricting or constraining thought comes into your mind, being big and expansive. You are thinking big, Mirabel, and you feel free and unfettered."

"What a marvelous feeling, Bella. I do feel free. Now all I have to do is think big when I approach my day."

"Don't 'have to,' Mirabel. That's another caged thought. Just be big as soon as you wake up in the morning. You know what to do. Let your imagination take flight during your day and watch how your daily tasks bend to the will of the master. You are in touch with that playful part of you. Mirabel, go to the rest of your day feeling big. We shall be around you, enjoying your newfound freedom."

"Thank you, Bella. This is most extraordinary—feeling expansive. What a difference it makes right now. I don't feel constricted. I'll see you around, Bella. Adios!"

"Adios, Mirabel. Have fun!"

Message: Everyone has mundane tasks, and you may have some that you feel are not worthy of your time. However, grant them worthiness. When you think big you give them room to be worthy components for the smooth running of your daily life.

Letting Your Cares Go: Never, Never Land

"Hello, Mirabel, come on! Come out to play!"

"Good morning, Bella. You are driving me nuts this morning. First you began pulling the bedclothes off me, then you began dancing in the kitchen, not to mention your pals making noise with all of the pots and pans. What's going on?"

"Well, Mirabel, you are in a stew this morning, and we want to get your attention, so let go of your stewing!"

"Very funny, Bella. Yes, I'm in a stew, and it's all house stuff encroaching on my peace. I just don't know which way to swing. And don't you dare to take off on one of your rambles! What's on your little mind this morning?"

"We want to take you on a journey."

"A journey? Okay, whatever you say."

"We do say. How about a journey to Never, Never Land?"

"I don't know if I trust you, Bella. Never, Never Land? What will you come up with next? You get goofier and goofier by the minute."

"Now, now, Mirabel, temper, temper. We are going to the land of little people, who know how to let their cares go."

"Well, I don't know about this. But I certainly could do with letting the house business go at the moment."

"Settle back and enjoy the ride, Mirabel. Letting your cares go is the ride we are going on. Your cares have taken possession of you, oh, golden one."

"Yes, I agree, Bella. Let's go for the ride. ... Oh, dear. I shouldn't have said that. There you are, off again. Now we are on roller coasters at a fair. That brings back memories, Bella. I used to love those high rides in the sky and sweeping down curves and rising up on others. It was exhilarating!"

"Yes, Mirabel, that memory took you back to happier times. You were free. How does it feel with the wind rushing through your hair, and hanging on for dear life to the bars of the car as you go up and then down on the big wheel? Fun, wasn't it?"

"Yes, it was. But how is this related to letting my cares go, or have you gone off on one of your tangents?"

"No, we are just getting you started on the ride to Never, Never Land. Just think, Mirabel, about how free you felt on that roller coaster ride. Wouldn't you like to feel that free again?"

"Now, Bella, how can I feel that free again when I'm so encumbered with responsibility?"

"Oh, dear, we are feeling sorry for ourselves. Whatever happened to the funny Mirabel we enjoy playing with?"

"Bella, you've turned into a big, black figure. What are you telling me?"

"That's you right now, Mirabel—a big, black, somber figure, all weighed down with chains and balls, all of your responsibilities."

"Bella, I can't look that bad!"

"Yes, you do, Mirabel. Come on outside and play with us."

"I guess I have no choice. ... Okay, I'm ready to play."

"Good, that's better. Where shall I begin? Ah, yes. First, Never, Never Land. Let's just fly there, Mirabel. Take my hand!"

"If you say so. I know I did this once before flying with you. Let's go.... Wow! This is beautiful! We are traveling all around the earth. I see tiny villages, snow-capped mountains. Didn't we travel this route before, Bella?"

"No, not quite the same. However, we will smash through the sound barrier any minute now!"

"What? Wait a minute! You didn't tell me we would be doing that!"

"What of it? Just relax, Mirabel. Trust me. Are you ready to take off?"

"I'm closing my eyes and hanging on for dear life! … Where are we, Bella? All of sudden I was flying, and now I have firm ground under my feet!"

"Yes, Mirabel. We can move in the twinkling of an eye to a place of our choosing. You can open your eyes now."

"This is a very strange place. I see in the distance lots and lots of people moving around, doing things. Where are we?"

"We are in Never, Never Land, Mirabel. This is the place where you will see how people let their cares go. This is a little village on the outskirts of a large city. We wanted you to experience the energy here."

"It does feel different—the energy. Why, Bella?"

"Just observe, Mirabel."

"I am. I observe people talking. Others are reading, and still others are conducting business; the latter I see though the windows of the homes. There are no office buildings, Bella. Do people conduct business in their home?"

"This is a satellite village, Mirabel. It's an experiment. All the residents are working on some project or other, and through their technology they combine their findings. No one individual works on his or her own. They work as a team. Their project right now is teaching earthlings how to let go of their cares. This was set up when it was feared many decades ago that technology would enslave humans. What do you say to that, Mirabel?"

"I'm astonished! I do understand what you say that humans become slaves to their technology. It's so easy to become trapped. But how does letting go of your cares enter into this?"

"Well, you observed that some villagers are reading while others are going about their business. Those readers are energetically connected to the workers. If the workers become too involved with their projects, the readers pull on an invisible string that is attached to the workers' hearts to remind them to let go."

"What happens next?"

"See for yourself, Mirabel."

"Very strange. I see the workers who have had a tug on their hearts stop, walk away, and spend time at the window or walking outside to enjoy the scenery, or just getting a cup of coffee. Others are talking to an associate. One is actually running his hands through his hair; he's so wired up. What does it all mean, Bella?"

"The one who is 'wired up,' as you say, has become too involved with his project. He's in the process of untangling his energy from the project's energy. Mirabel, do you understand that your beautiful energy becomes taut when you allow your responsibilities to take over? The responsibilities begin the process of eroding your freedom. They have a life, you know. So many of you mortals are not aware of the energy involved in your projects or things. But you, Mirabel, are aware. So, we thought it was high time you saw what happens when you get stuck in the mud! Time for your break Mirabel. We will be here when you get back."

* * * * * * * * * *

"I'm back, Bella, but I'm a little disoriented."

"Oh, well, we will have to do something about that."

"Bella, you're standing on my head, and one of your pals is standing on my feet. What do you hope to accomplish?"

"Wait and see what God sends you! Ha-ha!"

"Bella, ... what are you up to? I don't trust you. Oh, my head is getting heavier and heavier. It's getting too heavy for my body. And my feet, they're glued to the ground. Oh, I feel my energy descending down to my feet. Wow, that's a neat trick, Bella!"

"No trick, Mirabel. We are grounding you, pushing your energy into the earth. My pals on your feet are diving into the earth with it. Can you see what they are doing?"

"Yes, they are anchoring it to a solid rock. The rock is emanating its thanks for being of service. It's welcoming me by embracing me with its energy. ... Bella, I'm about to cry. This is so incredible!"

"Just stay anchored there for a moment, Mirabel, while the rock is soothing you in its embrace and taking away your cares. When you walk away from your cares, even for five minutes, the earth is ready to embrace them. You have lovely rocks, Mirabel. Make patterns with them. Or hold them occasionally. They are your friends. They came to you with a specific purpose. You were not aware of that, were you?"

"Not really. It's as if all that information was on the periphery of my mind, but I didn't quite grasp it. It was foggy. ... I feel very free right now, Bella. But can we go back to the village? I want to see what's going on."

"Certainly. ... Do you see hearts being tugged by the invisible thread from the readers? This village is an experiment. All of the residents are volunteers on the project of 'Letting Your Cares Go.' They are monitoring their hearts, their thinking processes, their willingness to put down their tools and walk away. Many of them were on the earth plane and left it through tiredness and disillusionment with their toys, Mirabel. They didn't take time out to enjoy the splendors of the earth plane or to partake of its nourishing restfulness. They said they were too busy. Rather sad, don't you think?"

"Yes, it is sad. So, you saw me getting too involved. I understand. You're telling me to walk away when things get to me, or to put down the tools when my mind is becoming overwhelmed."

"Yes Mirabel, and its lunchtime. Go outside and enjoy your garden and the bright sun. I see you are still fascinated with the village?"

"Yes, Bella. What happens at the heart level when the workers don't listen to it?"

"We'll show you!"

"Oh, no, what am I in for?"

"You asked for it, Mirabel. Here goes. We will have fun—right up our alley!"

"Hearts everywhere! They're encrusted with families, friends, gadgets, and more and more stuff. Bella, this is too much!"

"Just think for a moment, Mirabel. Your heart has to compete with all of this stuff pulling on you for attention. Its purpose is to love, not to be buried with what you think is love—love of all your trinkets! And love of all your demanding families and friends and constantly sweeping up after them. It doesn't have a chance to waft its love to you. No wonder it gives up and returns to its spirit home. It becomes tired of all the nonsense."

"Really, Bella, 'nonsense'? How can you say that? We do have responsibilities. What are we supposed to do? Walk away from them?"

"Yes, Mirabel! Walk away! Take a break. Release the hold they have on you. Then you can step back and observe your wanting to get everything done, getting it right. Now it's time for me to let go and walk away. I'm off to the sunlight. Time for my refreshment. Mirabel, you are now grounded and freed up from your cares. Come, join me in the garden and feel the sun on your face. Au revoir, oh, golden one."

"Okay, Bella. Just when I was becoming interested in this village, you close up shop! Au revoir, Bella."

Message: When you become so enamored of your things and your families and friends to the detriment of your heart's message of love, your heart becomes tired with so much competition. You are asked to consider its wistful desire to be only love.

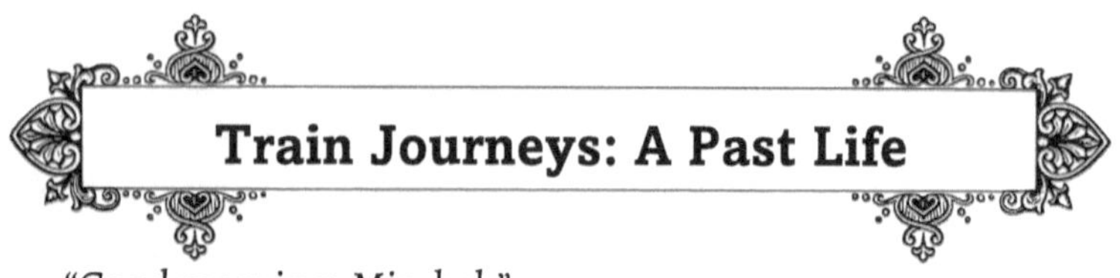

Train Journeys: A Past Life

"Good morning, Mirabel."

"Good morning, Bella. You've been charging around me for the last hour. What is it you want to speak to me about?"

"Oh, something very special, Mirabel. We see you becoming too focused on your house right now, and we thought it was time you had a break. We love the colors you have chosen for our space together. ... I know you don't want to talk about train journeys. However, any suggestion I give you gets shot down. You just don't believe we can use any description for a great message."

"Yes, I agree with you. I am always astonished when you come up with something. ... Oh, dear, you and your pals have changed into the kids' Thomas the Tank Engine and its buddies! What next? Are you taking me back to my childhood again, Bella?"

"No, Mirabel. We are using a train journey to explain something to you. Visualize yourself on a train, Mirabel. What does it do? And where is it going?"

"Okay, I'm visualizing myself on a train in Ireland. I have just managed to catch it. I had to run for it. I see myself sitting with two friends. We always sat together. Where is this conversation going, Bella?"

"Patience, Mirabel. Think about your life. Is it not like a train journey? Are you not always going somewhere, stopping at stations, getting off at a final destination?"

"Yes, I see what you're getting at. Let's go, then."

"Okay, oh, golden one. Think of your life on this beautiful planet as a series of train journeys. As you ride a train, you look out the window and see the scenery rushing by. This is your life, Mirabel. Sit for a moment and think about the present journey. Metaphorically, you are looking at life through the windows of your mind and thinking about experiencing some new challenge. Sometimes you pass up a challenge in favor of staying on the train and continuing on with your journey to the next station. That next station stop may be the end of your present experience. You are about to get off at a station and take a break, enjoy the scenery, meet new people, and enjoy their companionship. These journeys are about your lessons, Mirabel. Let's bring up one such journey."

"Oh, Bella, I guess I am in for it!"

"My, my, we are gloomy this morning, Mirabel!"

"You know, you're right. I am. I guess it's because I'm still without my usual space to work in. I miss the comfort of my cozy corner. This weekend it should be finished, and I can return to it."

"Cheer up, Mirabel. We can be around you anywhere. But you are a creature of habit, and you feel you can't write anywhere else except in your 'cozy corner'!"

"You have a point, Bella, but don't go off on a tangent on me. Let's continue with the train journey. I just got off at a station. It's beautiful?"

"We dressed up at the station for you, Mirabel. Do you like all the garlands of roses and flowerpots? This was your destiny on one such journey. So, you were greeted with joy, and the ticket master beamed upon you. You see, you completed a particularly arduous journey. You cleared a thicket of ambivalence that had bothered you for some time. This was a buried hurt. You brought it up for healing, and now you are greeted by all of your angelic friends who cheered you on, especially when the way became stony and treacherous. The ticket master is handing you a ticket for your next train journey. He brings you into a beautiful garden where there is a banquet prepared for you. Your angelic friends join you. It's a fun time, Mirabel. Be free, let go of any restraints on your heart, and sing with joy. You have earned this banquet."

"This is beautiful, Bella, but I'm a bit confused. Why all the fuss?"

"Mirabel, as we said, you have just completed a particularly rough. Journey. Don't you believe you deserve to be rewarded for all of your efforts?"

"Oh, I see what you mean. You're telling me I should celebrate after completion of a journey?"

"Yes, Mirabel. We see you mortals rushing headlong into new experiences without taking stock of those you just completed. It's as if you become intoxicated with the experience and forget to congratulate yourself on your achievements. You are eating chocolate but don't taste it, because you are so eager for more. Like the train journeys, in your enthusiasm you jump on to the next train you see, and sometimes you catch the wrong one, or forget to get off, and you wonder why everything has turned topsy-turvy on you!"

"You're losing me, Bella. And stop dancing around. You're making me dizzy!"

"Just trying to jazz things up a bit, Mirabel. We don't want to take you too seriously. Actually, I think I will have a jazz band play for us!"

"Oh, no, there you go—you and your pals. And you look ridiculous. The instruments are bigger than you. What will you dream up next, Bella?"

"That's it, Mirabel. That's it!"

"What is it, Bella? What are you trying to tell me?"

"Dreams, Mirabel. Get off the train and dream for a while. You mortals are handed gifts of rest, and what do you do? You fret! Ha! What is the point of doing all the hard work if you become so infatuated with your creations that you forget to take time out and explore your world? Each station serves as a market for you, Mirabel. Do you want to explore it, or do you want to continue the journey? Do you want to finish the present journey? Are you ready to jump off the train and say good-bye to that last lesson? Or have you decided to stay on board until your time is up here on this beautiful planet? I don't think you are ready for that yet, Mirabel."

"No, I'm not. I still want to explore other journeys. ... Where are you off to now, Bella?"

"Just planning on taking you for a ride. Jump onto my train!"

"I'm nervous about this, Bella. What are you up to? ... For goodness' sake, you and your pals have changed into a train and are beckoning me to climb aboard. You'd better shrink me down to size, Bella."

"We will do that, Mirabel. ... See? You are now the size of an ant. Climb aboard, Mirabel. We are going on a train journey into dreamland."

"Really? I guess I'd better be prepared. ... We're moving too fast, Bella! Slow down!"

"No, Mirabel. You mortals fly like this down your highways in your outlandish automobiles, oblivious to everything around you. You don't even see the sky or the landscape. You are all too busy gobbling up the highway as fast as you can."

"Mmm, I see what you mean, Bella."

"You are a fast mover, Mirabel, and we enjoy your speed. We ride on your aura, and it's fun to feel the wind rushing through our wings."

"Mmm, I didn't know that."

"Yes, Mirabel, we do enjoy you, oh, golden one. You look at the sky when you stop at traffic lights; you admire the trees and the grass and send out blessings to your fellow travelers. Your journeys are filled with little pleasures. You may be crestfallen or in doubt, but you enjoy the blessed gifts nature has to offer you. Even still, you avoid another journey when you feel in doubt or are afraid it will be too hard."

"You are so right, Bella. ... I see we have arrived at a station. You and your pals are dancing on my aura again. Where are we, Bella?"

"Waiting for a change of trains for your next destination, Mirabel. Isn't this 'neat,' as you mortals say?"

"Yes, this station is weird. It keeps changing shape. It's as if it's alive. ... It is! Tell your pals to quit having fun with me, Bella. Why would you do that?"

"We don't want you to become fixed on one idea, Mirabel. Just think of the hundreds of possibilities you have at this station."

"It's too much for my brain, Bella. What am I supposed to be doing here?"

"Why don't you look around you, Mirabel, and choose one idea you would like to pursue—maybe a train journey back to the Library of Records and look into a past life. That would be fun, wouldn't it? To see what you did in another life?"

"I don't know about that, Bella. Anytime I looked at a past life, it was usually pretty awful. That wouldn't be my cup of tea."

"Well, we'll find a fun one for you. Let's take a journey to the Library of Records and look up a past life. The master librarian will loan us your big book of records."

"Oh, boy, here we go. ... Really, Bella, that book is huge. It's taking you and several of your pals to carry it to a table' and they're having a spirited discussion about what past life to choose. Mmm, I wonder where this is going."

"Okay, Mirabel. We have found a life where you had lots of fun. Come and see."

"I don't believe it. Why would you find such a past life when I couldn't?"

"Well, the past lives you chose were lives in which you decided to learn spiritual skills, and you incorporated them into all of your future lives. … Here we are. Guess what time period, Mirabel."

"Let me see a picture. Oh, my! All the words have changed into people, and I'm in the middle of a crowd of them laughing and dancing. I'm dancing?"

"Yes, you are, Mirabel. In that life you were a dancer, and although you weren't rich, you were famous. See your beautiful dress? Can you guess the country and the time period?"

"On checking the scenery, it looks like a time period in Greece. I remember, I did have a life in Greece, and I was very happy. I was loved by my family, and I was my father's favorite child. I danced for the religious festivals and in the Temple of Athena. I see myself dancing a dance with veils; it was my own creation. I was very light on my feet and could leap through the air twirling the veils and making beautiful patterns with them. Sometimes I imitated a bird using two veils for wings, or other dancers would pull the veils out from me and dance around me in a circle, while I twirled like a spinning top in the center. I feel I'm right back there, Bella."

"That's because you carry the memory of those dance steps in your cells, Mirabel. Your body remembers them whenever you put on Greek music and dance to it."

"Yes, I love the Greek dances. Oh, Bella, you have given me so much to think about. … I know, I know. I see you shaking your head I won't think. I'll have fun reminiscing. I would like to stay here for a while and just enjoy the scenes as they pass before my eyes."

"Okay, Mirabel, we will leave you here. We will take you back to your earth when you catnap. You will wake up refreshed and in joy. Au revoir! Have fun."

"Au revoir, Bella, and thank you for this enchanting experience."

Message: All of your life experiences are like train journeys. Each train journey represents a value learned, an adversity overcome, a manifestation of a dream, or the fun times and the hard times. Many lessons are forgotten, but you can remember them by taking time out to reminisce and enjoy the fruits of your labor.

Fun

"Good morning, Mirabel."

"Good morning, Bella. What's in store for me this morning?"

"Fun!"

"This should be interesting. Tell me why this subject?"

"We thought we would jazz you up a bit. Have some fun with you!"

"Oh, dear, here we go. What are you dreaming up in that little head of yours?"

"Wait and see, Mirabel!"

"All right, but don't wait too long. I might get bored!"

"Ah-ha, that's it—boredom!"

"What is it? And how does boredom factor in?"

"If you infused your daily tasks and activities with some fun, Mirabel, they wouldn't be boring or tiresome, or a 'drag.' Isn't that what you mortals say?"

"Yes, some of us love the 'drag' word."

"Mmm, now, that's a nice picture, a drag."

"Bella?"

"Yes, oh golden one?"

"Too late—you're at it again. What are you supposed to be?"

"A picture of a drag."

"If you must, carry on, but I wouldn't call that a drag."

"Ah, well, I was just having some fun. I'll settle for some wit instead."

"Now I'm puzzled."

"Let's get the show on the road, Mirabel. Pretend you are in a traveling circus. You are one of the clowns, all dressed up in baggy, multicolored pants, a blousy top, and you have a huge red nose. Your hat reaches a good three feet! You do look bizarre!"

"You're being funny. Are you joining me too? You look like a tiny buffoon—and get off my nose!"

"You are a stick in the mud! I will try a different tack. Let me see."

"Now you're blowing up into your professor mode. Okay, I guess I'm in for it."

"Fun, Mirabel, how does it feel to you?"

"Light and air-filled!"

"Yes, Mirabel, you laugh at your little mistakes and your foibles all the time. You will agree with me, won't you, that it takes the sting out of them?"

"Yes, it does. I remember laughing the other day in a restaurant when I couldn't find my hat. It was in my pocket all the time."

"Mirabel, do you recall when you were a teenager, walking into the men's room for the first time? You ran out mortified at your mistake!"

"Yes, I do. Today I wouldn't be fazed by that at all. I would chuckle and take it in stride."

"Keep going. What other funny memories do you have?"

"Mmm, let me think a minute."

"Let me help you."

"What are you doing, Bella? You've turned into a huge head with several eyes, and one of the eyes has a door in it. Grotesque!"

"Peep in through that doorway, Mirabel. What do you see?"

"Must I?"

"Yes!"

"Okay, okay, keep your shirt on! I'm looking at an old memory, Bella. I see a girlfriend from school standing on a chair and scraping off stew from the kitchen ceiling. It was so hilarious, my sides ached from laughing. She was angry with me for laughing at her. I finally pulled myself together and helped her clean up the mess. before her mother came home. My friend had used a pressure cooker for the first time, but she didn't read the instructions! We both succumbed to giggling again.

"That brings back another memory, Bella. I had been married for just a couple of months, and my husband invited a friend to dinner. I was very proud of myself; everything was perfect. The chicken was cooking in the pressure cooker, the vegetables were steaming, and the table was set with Irish linen and my good china and silverware. While my husband and his friend chatted, I checked the dinner. The chicken was done, and everything was ready. However, I couldn't get the lid off the pressure cooker. I panicked. I had to ask my husband to help me. The lid wouldn't budge. It took him and his friend armed with a chisel and hammer to get it off! When they finally did, the chicken had shriveled to the size of a tennis ball. What a disaster! I was so humiliated, I wanted to die. We had snacks and salad for dinner."

"Yes, Mirabel, you did. However, at many parties later, you told your friends about that catastrophe, and it was the source of much laughter. Your friends chimed in with similar stories and the wine flowed!"

"Yes, indeed, they were good times. Sometimes I feel I have lost some of that lightheartedness. Perhaps it is because I have grown older. ... Bella, your eyes are tearing up."

"You have become sad, Mirabel. My pals are skating up and down your aura to get you back on even keel. Don't be sad. That is why we came to you today. We want you to have fun with all of your days. Find fun in everything you do, Mirabel. Put on that folk music that has a real stomping beat and grab your loving spouse and dance around the kitchen with him."

"You are around me a lot. I thought you spent most of your time in the garden."

"Yes, we do. However, we love your golden company."

"Bella, you've set me off thinking about the many times I've laughed at the silliest things. Even now I remember walking to the village in the old country and my under-slip began falling down because the elastic had snapped. I tried hitching it up, but the material was silky. Eventually I just ducked behind a tree and stepped out of it. Mind you, I didn't think it was funny at the time, but now I do."

"Come up to the present time, Mirabel. Where are your silly moments now?"

"Ah, Bella, now I know what you're getting at. There haven't been too many silly moments lately. My husband and I have both allowed ourselves to be cluttered up with house projects."

"Yes, you have. However, you could have brought some fun into those areas. You could have put up a big notice in your office saying, 'This is the space of Her Imperial Highness. Enter at your peril!' Or when you couldn't find anything amid all of your careful packing, you could have used a paper trail."

"You are so right, Bella. I used to put a paper trail all over the house when the budget money was due. Each page had something written on it: 'MONEY TIME,' 'COUGH UP,' 'THE BUDGET IS DUE.' My husband would conveniently forget, hoping he could hold on to his money for another day. It was always a source of laughter between us. We would both indulge in a verbal sparring match to see which one of us would come up with the wittiest statement. He usually won. That's how it was all the time: find fun in something and—poof—we're off on a sparkling verbal duel!"

"Mirabel, that is we why we love to be around you. You should see the sparks emanating from your aura when you and your loved one are battling one another in good fun. We watched with glee. Then we take your laughter and bring it out to the garden to feed your plants. We tell them it is a gift from Mirabel. But your house projects have drained your energy, oh, golden one. You push too hard to get them done. You both forgot to laugh. Ah, and then your back brought you down!"

"You are correct, my little friend. When I strained my back, I had no choice but to sit down and rest. Boy, did it hurt. ... Wait a minute, Bella. You said you took my laughter out to the garden to feed the plants. How can you do that? The more I think about it, the more I find it farcical!"

"Yes, it is farcical Mirabel. However, oh golden one, all humans bring healing to plants when they are laughing with joy. That energy revs up their gears."

"Now you are being funny. I think it's time we closed this conversation, but I will remember it."

"Do that, Mirabel, and reminisce today on all the funny incidences in your life. They bring a smile to your face and energize you. Adios, my golden friend."

"Adios, Bella."

Message: Bringing the gift of laughter and silliness into your life when you become bored with your daily routine will do much to invigorate and uplift you.

Secrets of the Plant World

"Hello there, Mirabel."

"Hello, Bella."

"Look out your window, Mirabel. What do you see? We would like to usher in the bright colors of spring!"

"And pray, how are you going to do that? And what can you say about spring that I don't already know?"

"Wait and see, Mirabel. As of now, you are drifting into a gentle sleepiness. You have been doing this lately, Mirabel, and we are noticing you are not vexed with yourself. This is one of the great awakenings of spring—mortals drifting into a gentle drowsiness. This is nature's way of getting mortals' attention. Spring has many healing aspects to it, Mirabel…. You are drifting, Mirabel. That is wonderful. Now we can take you on a journey down through the earth, where you can really see spring in all of its glory! Gentle drifting, Mirabel."

"Bella, this is beautiful! I see a carpet of green stretching for miles, and there are many angelic beings talking to little devic creatures—those delightful tiny unseen workers that live in our gardens. What is happening, Bella?"

"You are in the land of the devic world, Mirabel. Feel the grass under your feet. It has a different texture, does it not?"

"Yes, it feels like velvet. I see groups of little devic children, too, with several angels. It's lovely, Bella. I see lots of flowering trees, daffodils, crocus, bluebells, and many other spring flowers. I also hear bees buzzing and the first blue bottles—those noisy flies! What is my lesson for today, Bella?"

"You are an eager beaver this morning, Mirabel."

"Yes, I am. I feel spring in my veins. It's flowing through me, and it energizes me, even though I want to doze off a lot. Why is that Bella?"

"You are a child of the earth, Mirabel, but you have forgotten this. One of your favorite universes to visit before you were born was the devic world. You delighted in the mischief of us little creatures. You also learned to plant. Seeds and care for them. Take a look around your physical garden, Mirabel. Is this not a creation of your deep love for plants and color? You learned that with us before you were born into the earth plane. However, we digress, Mirabel. Let us continue with the tour of our world."

"Oh, dear. You're blowing up into one of your modes of operation, Bella! ...Oh, my, you're a zucchini with arms, legs, and eyes. You do look funny!"

"This is one thing you loved about us here in our world—our ability to change into vegetables, fruits, trees, plants, flowers, and many other substances. You were fascinated and you spent many happy hours with us playing and dancing around us. Hasn't it occurred to you, Mirabel, to wonder why you are so comfortable with us?"

"Yes, it's dawning on me why I enjoy your company now, even though at times I get cross with you for distracting me. What's happened to our lesson?"

"All in good time, Mirabel. Enjoy the scenery, smell the flowers, the grass, listen to the bees and the blue bottles. And see if you can see rabbits and squirrels. They are not allowed into our garden when we are teaching or working with the plant world. That is our greatest asset to you mortals, Mirabel!"

"What is, Bella?"

"Let us show you. Take my hand, Mirabel, while we go underground to find our root friends and our bulb friends. … What do you see, Mirabel?"

"Good gracious, Bella. I see hundreds of little workers, cleaning bulbs, inspecting them, and still others checking trays on long tables. Some of the workers are spraying the trays with some kind of solution. What's happening, Bella?"

"Mirabel, the spraying is a concoction of special energy. It looks like liquid, but it is not. It is a fluid energy that has within its elements of the stars, nutrients necessary for the creation of a species of flower. It forms a cocoon around a seed. Then an angelic worker using its hands spins a web of energy around the tray. Lastly it is infused with a special infrared light and left to incubate for several days in your human time. Others angelic beings are on the sidelines awaiting the sprouting of the seed. It is quite a process, Mirabel, wouldn't you agree?"

"I'm just taking it all in, Bella. I see some of the angelic beings are walking up and down between rows of trays. What are they doing, Bella?"

"Sometimes the formula is not correct for a species, and it has to be abandoned. That appears if the cocoon splits around the seeds. However, it is not discarded. It is lovingly and carefully detached from the cocoon and placed in a special solution that will allow it to return to its star system."

"Return to a star system, Bella? Now, you have me puzzled!"

"On full moon days in our kingdom, these faulty seeds are placed in a special area of our garden, and the full moon shrouds the little seeds and sends them on their way to the star system they came from. This is a very simple explanation, Mirabel. There is much more involved, such as crystals and discrete elements of a star system. But for now, we think you know enough."

"Mmm, you're holding back on me! But I don't think I want to know all the secrets anyway. I would miss what's going on in other parts of this magical garden."

"Rightly so, Mirabel. What do you make of these seedlings over here?"

"No idea, Bella. They look like ordinary plants to me, could be. Anything."

"They are the seedlings of the mighty oak tree."

"Oh, gosh, now you're growing into a huge, tall, oak tree. I can't talk to you at the top of the tree, Bella. Come down!"

"Yes, you can, Mirabel. Just think tall and be up here with me. It's a grand view from up here!"

"Be free, Mirabel. Fly up here if you don't want to feel tall."

"I guess I have no choice. Well, here goes. ... I'm closing my eyes and imagining myself growing tall. ... For heaven's sake, Bella. I'm like a bean pole. I can't even see my feet, and, besides, I get dizzy if I look down!"

"Stop complaining, Mirabel. Enjoy the view and have a cup of tea."

"Bella, you are becoming irascible! Wow! The view is marvelous!

Blue mountains in the distance and miles and miles of meadows with plants growing at different heights. Are these experimental gardens, Bella? Because I see little plots marked off with tags."

"Yes, those little plots are being made ready for transfer to your world, Mirabel. They are ready and willing to try their wings at living on Mother Earth. Their express wish is to bring joy. Now, are you ready to fly down to the roots of the mighty oak?" Okay, let's go, but I'm closing my eyes."

"Coward!"

"All right for you to say that, but you're not living in a physical body!"

"Hold my hand, Mirabel, and we will both float together down to the roots. Of this wonderful creation."

"You may open your eyes … we are there!"

"Wow, look at that network of roots! I can't see where they go, but they travel far and wide, right? I'm speechless."

"Mirabel, what you are looking at are strings of energy. Again, like seeds, they are growing in a special medium composed of all of the elements of their star system. In addition, they are shrouded in a cloud of green—what you call chlorophyll. Interspersed in chlorophyll are very fine, almost invisible, electrical substances that ignite periodically. Those tiny substances are stimulating the energy strings to form roots that will be transferred to your earth. Look around, Mirabel. What do you see?"

"It's a beautiful, light-filled laboratory. I now see other angelic beings working with other little energy strings. This is incredible, Bella. I also feel like sleeping; the atmosphere has that effect on me. I can hardly keep my eyes open."

"Relax, Mirabel, you are in a special environment. These tiny root systems are in the sleeping state of their growth. It will be quite some time before they emerge into your world. The atmosphere is euphoric in keeping with their resting state. You love this laboratory, Mirabel; you come here quite often. The atmosphere nurtures you and the angelic beings know you. Periodically one will stop and weave a net of joy around you. They know the work you are doing on the earth plane. … Are you ready to return to your earthly garden, Mirabel?"

"You know for once I want to stay. I guess it's because I know this place…. Ah, well, onward I will go. I'm ready, Bella. … Ah, you're back to your tiny self. Well, that's the signal that our little journey is over. Okay, Bella, wave your magic wand!"

"You can always come here in your imagination, Mirabel. Now that spring is on the way, go into your garden, look and listen. Au revoir, Mirabel."

"Au revoir, Bella."

Message: It can be enlightening to take a good look at the plant and insect world, especially in spring. Be aware of the roles being played by angelic. Beings who incubate all the matrix necessary for plant life on your earth. As you do, you will learn to view nature with a sense of wonder.

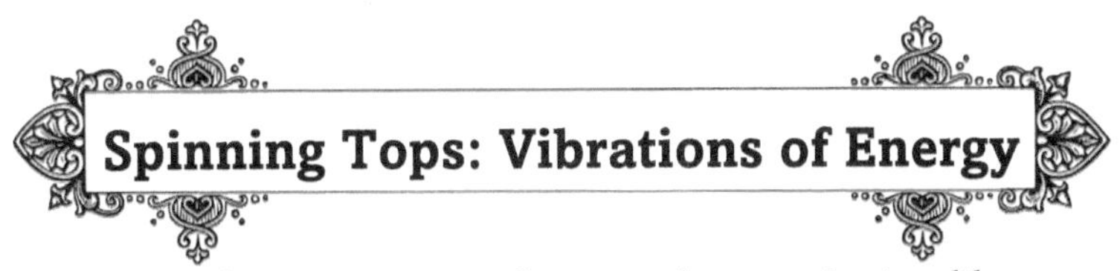

Spinning Tops: Vibrations of Energy

"Bella, what's up? You and your pals are spinning like tops. There are hundreds of you!"

"Good morning, Mirabel."

"Good morning, Bella. Mmm, are you keeping me in suspense this morning?"

"Yes, Mirabel, we are, all of us little devas. Do you feel that suspense, Mirabel? Can you picture yourself spinning like a top. Try it!"

"Okay, I know from past experience that if I don't, you'll pull a fast one on me. Here goes. ... This isn't easy, Bella. I'm trying to spin this body of mine, but it's too heavy. Incredible, I can see into it, all the organs, bones, and nervous system. It's quite a mass to spin, Bella. How do you expect me to spin this mass of mine?"

"Easy, Mirabel. Stop for a moment and watch us. ... Use your imagination, Mirabel. Pretend you are a tiny top. Now try it."

"Yes, I see what you mean, Bella. Imagining myself as a tiny top makes it much easier to spin. ... Wow, I'm getting dizzy! I'm moving so fast, Bella, I'm floating. It's effortless."

"Good. Now look at all of your cells, Mirabel. Are they spinning?"

"Yes, it's amazing. They look like millions of tiny sparkling lights winking on and off. Just to ask a simple question, Bella—what's the purpose of all this spinning?"

"You would have to spoil it, Mirabel. Just when we thought we got you going round and round and floating into outer space, you began thinking!"

"Well, you must admit I'm puzzled."

"Then let's pause a moment, Mirabel. We will spin some more for you and ask you—what does the spinning do for you?"

"Okay, I'm ready for a break. Spinning can be dizzying! ... Now what are you doing? You've grown into a tall, green, skinny bean stalk, and you're spinning totally out of control. You've taken off, roots and all. Where are you, Bella?"

"Not far away. Look around you. I have come to ground again."

"So, you have, and you're as flat as a pancake! Oh, dear, you've lost it this time."

"No, I haven't. Get into your spinning top mode again. ... How do you feel, Mirabel?"

"Wonderfully light and free."

* * * * * * * * *

"Get off my keyboard, Bella. I know I shouldn't have answered that phone call, but it was a family member! Now, where were we?"

"Huffy, huffy, Mirabel. I was having such fun dancing on the computer keys! Let me see. Where was I? Ah, yes. Spinning, Mirabel, brings you up to a very high speed of energy. In that high energy you can access other universes, but only those at the level at which you are spinning."

"You're kidding."

"No, I'm not. That is why we love to play around your aura, that lovely ethereal light around your body. It shimmers with light-filled energy. You healed all energy that was not uplifting or nurturing to your spirit. It took you many years of earth time. Are you with me so far, Mirabel?"

"Yes, I think so, but what has spinning got to do with it?"

"What we just said—spinning at high speed takes you out to other universes, but only those that spin at your rate. You cannot go higher until you learn to spin at a rate in synch with that universe. It is quite complicated, Mirabel. And we don't have the wherewithal to explain it to you in scientific terms. However, you can see the picture of what we are telling you."

"Mmm ... you have me thinking ... I know, you don't want me to think. However, I'm gleaning a picture of myself in those universes that I have accessed in the past through other spiritual work. And, yes, I learned spinning to do that. I should have thought there are souls who can do that at will, Bella."

"Yes, there are, Mirabel, but those souls have attained or came in with a very high rate of energy in order to do this. You came in with a very bright light. However, you had lessons to learn before your soul allowed you to soar."

"Very interesting! So what else is there about spinning that I should know?"

"Every earth being, Mirabel, spins at a certain vibratory rate—some low, some high. Those at the lower end of the vibration can only understand and access knowledge at that rate. They live in families of the same vibration and have like friends. As they mature on their spiritual earth journey, they automatically spin at a higher vibratory rate, thus accessing more knowledge and aligning themselves with those souls of the same vibratory rate. Some even walk away from their earth families, and it is a very lonely path for them. However, they come to see with their spirit eyes unseen guides around them. Like you, Mirabel, I came to you when you were in an altered state. We were waiting on the sidelines to play with you. You were ready for us, even though at the rational level you refused to believe it. You shooed us away, remember?"

"Yes, you're right, Bella. You have to admit it was quite a shock to me, seeing you for the first time. But we've come a long way since then. So, what you're saying is that those of us who have learned to spin at a high rate have access to a comparable vibration. In other words, we attract like souls to us and like experiences?"

"Yes, and even your cells, Mirabel, spin at very excited states. This enables them to slough off undesirable energy. It's like a spring cleaning!"

"Don't mention the word ... I'm way behind on that."

"Well, think 'spin,' Mirabel, and go into it and see it all being achieved with a swipe of your light card! Ha-ha, we got you there!"

"I think it's time to end this conversation. You're becoming silly!"

"Yes, we are. And you are getting too serious. Lighten up, Mirabel, spin a little. Besides, it's time for our play outside. The sun is shining, and we have much to do. Au revoir, Mirabel."

"Au revoir, Bella."

Message: Underneath your physical body are vibrations of energy. In order to increase your spin and reach a higher level of wisdom and light, it is necessary to heal all energy that is not uplifting or nurturing to yourself. This may necessitate walking away from family and friends.

The Magic of Spring

"Good morning, Bella." "Good morning, Mirabel."

"You've been buzzing around me talking to me about magic. Is this the content of our conversation this morning?"

"Why not, Mirabel? It's about time you thought about magic."

"I can't fathom what you will say about magic."

"Where's your imagination, your eyes, your ears, Mirabel?" "Hmm ... I wonder where you're going to go with this one."

"Well, try me. Let's start with the magic of spring."

"It's your ball, Bella. Carry on! ... Oh, heck, I shouldn't have said that. There you go, off on one of your goofy displays. I see your pals have joined you. ... Oh, my, you are all Ping-Pong balls dancing up and down ... and ... get off my head!"

"Now, now, Mirabel. Where's the funny you this morning?"

"A bit ragged around the edges, since you ask!"

"Well, let's get some magic going here, Mirabel. We shall be very grand for this one. I will go into my professor mode."

"Oh, dear. Yes, you're in your pompous, professor mode, and all your pals are lined up waiting for your orders."

"This calls for pompousness. We shall discuss the 'Rite of Spring.' Do you remember spring, Mirabel?"

"Of course, I do. I love spring—the daffodils, the fresh greenery, the singing birds."

"Ah, but there is more to it than that, Mirabel. The spring to us is a wondrous time. It is a time of renewal, of birth, of family gatherings, of dancing around the Maypole, of scattering the last shreds of winter, of claiming our gifts that lay dormant during winter, of preening our wings, and hundreds of other little things that spring rewards us with. What would you say about renewal, Mirabel?"

"Yes, I see what you mean—renewal, a time of renewing old acquaintances, reviving a forgotten skill, refreshing one's skills."

"Mmm, not bad, Mirabel. However, renewal is also a time of looking at one's life, of discarding old stuff that's never used anymore. But, more importantly, what does it do for the psyche? Do you feel a quickening of your spirits? Do you feel the warmth of the spring sun on your cheeks? What about the singing of the birds - do they not bring you joy?"

"I see what you mean about magic, Bella. Yes, it's magical at this time of the year. Everything is so fresh and green. Yes, it does bring a quickening to my spirit. I want to do things—garden, walk, have ice cream. Love is in the air. Why do we neglect to see magic in these familiar things, Bella?"

"Ah, well, now, that's a big subject, Mirabel! We sigh at you humans when spring emerges. We do all we can to get your attention. We are involved with the gorgeous variations of the color green. And green is so healing. We see more and more humans becoming aware of spring, now that your weather is topsy-turvy! You humans are waking up. You are beginning to realize that your springs have become very erratic, and they are shorter. It dismays some of you. Others, however, are still cackling into their contraptions. ... Yes, contraptions, Mirabel. We saw your expression. Those things are a menace. They were supposed to be used in times of necessity. They are never out of your hands - you are constantly talking into them!"

"Do I detect a note of annoyance in your voice, Bella?"

"Yes, you do. We are so anxious to get your attention at this time on your beautiful earth. It needs to be observed, to be admired, to be loved, to be nurtured. I heard that, Mirabel—yes, farmers do nurture the earth. But we are talking about ordinary humans taking notice of the beauty around them, of the magic in the air in springtime. Your earth, Mirabel, is calling out to you through its beauty, through its contrary weather patterns. We call out to you. See us, dance with us, play with us. We take care of the earth and all of its little creatures. We would love to play with your little children. They are magical when they take their first tottering steps, and humans are entranced with that. But they are limited in their enchantments. What do you have to say, Mirabel?"

"I'm breathless listening to you, Bella. ...However, I 'm way ahead of you. Last week I went out into the garden, sat and listened to the bees buzzing around the flowers on the hollies. I closed my eyes and imagined I was back at my old home in Ireland. I remember being fascinated with them when I was child. I loved the sound. I can hear them now."

"Mirabel, that is one of the reasons we love to be around you. You are tuned in. You can't get enough of nature, especially in the spring. You yearn for it. You fill yourself up with it. You are charging your batteries when you do this, Mirabel. You are literally charging the cells in your body. This is how you stay healthy. Mother Nature rejuvenates you. That's magic, Mirabel."

"You have awakened memories in me, Bella—the smell of hawthorn hedges, the daffodils, the apple blossoms, the green pastures, the family walks, the first hint of summer, and the morning sun streaming in the kitchen. Yes, it was magic. Are we really so unaware, Bella?"

"Yes, oh golden one. Humans are constantly rushing from one activity to another, never stopping to take in the healing colors and sounds of spring. If they did, their bodies would be refreshed. Their hearts would breathe in the joy of renewal, of hope."

"Oh, Bella, you're making me sad. Yes, I do love and feel the spring intensely. I can't get enough of it. Watching the birds, the animals, checking the new growth on plants, nurturing them with nutrients. They are my friends."

"Yes, Mirabel, they are. And we take care of them during the long winter days, making sure they are resting and building up their strength for their spring ball!"

"Spring ball?

"Look at the flowers of spring in all of their vibrant and delicate hues. They are dancing in the wind; they nod their little heads at the warming sun. You cannot see them, Mirabel, but they dance with joy. It is magic to them to show off their dainty petals, their jaunty hats, their profusion of shapes and sizes. Each flower dances in the wind. The bluebells are magic to watch. Their dresses are studded with tiny diamonds. They sparkle as they dance. It's magic, Mirabel, magic!"

"Bella, you have shown me for a second the dancing flowers. The bluebells are exquisite. This is beautiful! What more can I say? I'm really jazzed up for spring!"

"Good, good, Mirabel, because we are off to your garden to dance with the flowers and the birds and the animals. Au revoir, golden one."

"Au revoir, Bella."

Message: Spring is an exquisite time of the year, when everything is fresh and sparkling. It is a time of renewal. Kick off your shoes and walk on the fresh grass, hear the bees, the song of the birds, and enjoy the scent of the flowers. It's magical!

The Carpet Bag

"Hello, Mirabel. You had a grand time on vacation, didn't you?"

"Yes, I did, Bella, and good morning to you. I met some of your friends out west, too. But you have a message for me this beautiful day?"

"Yes, we do, Mirabel. The carpet bag—where is it? This is your bag of treasures. What have you done with it?"

"I don't know. I know it's around somewhere. ... Ah, there it is. It looks awfully dusty and dirty. Oh, my, I have neglected it. I have so much to remember these days, it's not surprising my treasure trove is in this sorry state!"

"Yes, oh, golden one. We thought to make you aware of its condition.

Let's see if we can open it. ... No, it's stuck.

"Look at you all. All lined up with oil cans with ridiculously long spigots. That's ludicrous! You only need to oil the lock."

"Ah-ha, that's not what you need. All of your joints need oiling! Pretend you are getting all of your joints oiled, Mirabel."

"Are you meandering again Bella? However, on musing what you said, oiling my joints is a great idea, but what happened to the treasure trove?"

"Patience, patience, Mirabel. Now that we have opened the bag, watch what happens!"

"It's spreading out like a carpet, and it has all sorts of toys, books, walks, bicycling, movies, chocolate, and fun things to do and play with. I get your drift."

"You have forgotten to take out this treasure trove and play with one of your toys when you feel dispirited. We'll select one for you. How about this book on the ancient Romans?"

"Oh, my gosh, I forgot about that book. It's one of my favorites. ... What are you doing, Bella? All of your pals have entered the book and are now little, tiny Roman soldiers all marching. Okay, what are you telling me?"

"We are not trying to tell you anything, Mirabel. Just have fun. Do you remember fun?"

"I must say you all look weird. You are so tiny, and one of the generals— or is that Caesar? —is dragging his cloak on the ground, and it appears he is lauding his troops, who have settled down into long marching lines. ... Oh, the scene has changed. What are you hunting for now?"

"Just a little something to jog your memory."

"You have turned into a big black key. What is this supposed to mean. I don't recall any black key."

"Think again, Mirabel, you did have such a key, but you have forgotten this, too. We'll help you out: it's a symbolic key!"

"Oh, I wonder what of? I don't get it! Now you've disappeared. It's all black and silent. In the distance I hear a thunderous sound. I recognize that sound and I hear your tinkling sound, too. Ah, the loud sound is the earth's tone, which I love to tune into when I need grounding. I see a group of Tibetan monks sitting in a circle echoing the earth's tone. Wow, it's powerful. Oh, Bella, I have been remiss. I've been so busy feeling sorry for myself and my injured left foot. ... Now, don't go there."

"Mm, a pity. Aw well, we just want to get your full attention."

"Well, you have it now. Let's go back to the other treasures that are on the carpet. I see you pulling out a huge bar of chocolate. Do I need that much?"

"Yes, this is to sweeten you up. You have been too preoccupied with your book."

"Now you've turned into a huge book, and all of your pals are dancing on the pages that are flying out to the universe. This is interesting."

"Your messages are being picked up by millions of humans, Mirabel." "Now, that's going too far. I don't believe it!"

"Oh, heck, the book has closed, and it has a little lock on it. What did I say?"

"You were disparaging of your work. So, we closed it. Since you didn't believe in it, no one else will."

"Oh, dear, what have I done? How do I undo this, Bella? ...And now you've blown up into a somber judge. I guess I asked for that."

"Smile, oh, golden one. Look what we found in your treasure trove!"

"It's another key—a golden one this time—and you're unlocking the book. I feel better already."

"Yes, you do. We also have another key. It is special. It unlocks the door to your inner, quiet, serene self. This is your private dwelling place. It has everything you need. Sometimes you forget this treasure, so we will tweak you occasionally as a reminder."

"You're changing again, Bella. You had me sobered up for a minute, and now you are all dancing jigs and reels. I also saw a tiny violinist. This is fun!"

"Yes, fun, never forget fun. It lightens up your life. It brings laughter to your heart, and it draws us to play with you, but now it's time for lunch. Go outside and enjoy the bees and the butterflies. We will send you lots of playmates to make you smile. Your heart is now opened, and your whole body is dancing to the rhythm of the music. We are off, Mirabel. Au revoir. See you outside!"

"Au revoir, Bella."

Message: When you become too preoccupied with your progress in life, seek out those things that uplift your spirits, chocolate, a good book—and enter that inner, quiet, serene self that has everything you require for your well-being.

Freedom

"Good morning, Bella."

"Good morning, Mirabel. Long time no see! We have been around you, but you have had your head in a can."

"Excuse me? What do you mean by that?"

"Just that, Mirabel. You seem to think the whole world is in your head, and you go fishing in it for ideas, goals, plans, and all sorts of stuff."

"I'm not sure what you're talking about. Of course, I would have to use my mind to flesh out ideas, plans, or goals. You make it sound so confining, as if there is nowhere else for me to go."

"Well, think about it, Mirabel. You have hemmed yourself in with one big topic—you!"

"I don't get this. I must be dimwitted this morning. Could you be a bit more explicit?"

"Sure, oh, golden one. Every time you become absorbed with one topic, you become immersed in it to the exclusion of everything else around you. Do you get the picture?"

"Yes, I do. Where does you part come in? I organize my days and accomplish what I can for that day."

"You are dim this morning, Mirabel. It has everything to do with it. The whole world is closed out while you have your head in a can."

"You said that before, Bella. ...And for gosh sakes, what are you doing? You and your pals are all cans with legs. I'm not commenting on this. Let's stick with the topic. You still haven't explained to me what it's all about."

"You are wound so tight right now, Mirabel, that your jaw is clenched. We know you have been struggling with the editing of our sprightly conversations. Couldn't you at least acknowledge that you have assistance all around you. I heard that 'Yes, but ...' No excuses, Mirabel. We see all the areas you are working in, and we have scratched our little heads wondering when you will put down the tools of labor and come outside and play. Yes, I know, the weather has been cold and wet. But you know what I mean, Mirabel. What happened to the trips to the library, your trips into the city for tea and browsing the bookstores?"

"You're right, Bella. I do miss my little excursions into the city, and especially the bookstores, not to forget the sheer joy of being free for a morning."

"Ah, yes, Mirabel. Freedom—that is your real struggle."

"Oh, you are so right, Bella. I feel I am hemmed in right now. I see all the projects ahead of me, and I'm asking myself, 'Do I really want to do this?' ... What are you up to now, Bella? You and your pals are jumping up and down on big red balls. Stop! It's making me dizzy."

"Just trying to be funny. You remember FUN, Mirabel?"

"Now you're being sarcastic."

"My apologies, oh, golden one. We miss you. When we have your attention, we know we are doing our part in your great earth life journey. When you play with us or even dance with us, we have a sense of déjà vu. We are delighted. You are one mortal in touch with the little beings of light in your world. So, we delight in that. Haven't you noticed how your garden glows in spring, which is around the corner, by the way?"

"I never knew you had a part in my journey here. This is a surprise, Bella. What else don't I know? And, yes, I have noticed how gorgeous the garden is in spring. I thought that was the same for everyone."

"No, not necessarily. There is a difference, Mirabel. We play in your garden and nourish it. Last year you cried in your garden because of the damage done by a member of the insect world. That was caused by the infusion of a certain liquid, the energy of which was unsuited for the life of your garden. Your garden, Mirabel, is protected by a shield of gold, but when an unnatural substance is introduced, it creates havoc."

"So that's what happened! I have already remedied the situation. But where were we, Bella?"

"You're sensing spring around the corner, Mirabel. This feeling is wanting you to give up everything you are doing. You want to stretch your wings and fly away. This has been your dilemma ever since you discovered what it is really like to be free."

"Yes, you're right. I'm having a tug-of-war with myself right now. ... Now you're all playing a tug-of-war with my aura. What's the idea?"

"Just straightening you out. You need to be unwound right now, Mirabel. Let go of all of your silly projects."

"They are not silly. They mean something to me and others. Anyway, haven't we gotten away from the topic?"

"Temper, temper. Now, let me see ... what was the topic?"

"Bella, no more games, I'm getting hungry!"

"Stay cool Mirabel, cool!"

"Now where was why? .... What would you do if you gave up all of your activities and projects? No cheating—right off the top of your head, Mirabel."

"Right now, I would drop everything and go out for the day. However, I'm searching for balance. I enjoy all that I do, but there's a part of me saying, 'Enough already.' It wants to be freed up to just laze around occasionally. I guess it's wanting to let go of having to do something all the time. I need your help with this, Bella."

"Well, now, Mirabel. Do you know how long we have waited for you to ask for our help?"

"You have? It would never have occurred to me!"

"Go to your lunch, Mirabel; you are hungry. Drop all your projects, put the tools away for the rest of the day, and allow spring to nourish you. Be free, Mirabel."

"I will, Bella. Au revoir and thank you."

Message: When you become so immersed in your projects to the point of not being able to let go, it is time to take a day off. When the sounds of spring call to you, allow yourself the freedom to drop everything and take time out to nourish your spirit.

Unknown Territory

"We are back again, Mirabel. Good afternoon to you."

"Good afternoon, Bella."

"Goodness, Mirabel! You do get yourself into messy tangles at times. You know this. You do not look ahead when you trot off on one of your jaunts into unknown lands! Check your compass and find your heart bearings and decide if that particular jaunt is right for you. What will it produce for you? What are the requirements? Are we on track so far?"

"Yes, you are."

"But more importantly, oh, golden one, you have not consulted your heart. When you allow your heart into the conversation with you, then a whole different picture opens up. Part of your dilemma is your empathy for others. You love assisting others on their journeys. Indeed, you sometimes bend over backward for them. You love to see them set free from their unwise entanglements. This is your creative nature working at full sail. In doing this, where have you set down rules to combat fatigue and allow yourself some lazy time and, more importantly, when to let go of others who come to you for guidance?"

"My goodness, Bella, you are right. Founts of wisdom from such a little creature!"

"Be careful, Mirabel, we might just pull a fast one on you. We might turn you inside out and show you just how the workings of the mind affect your body."

"Please, don't do that, Bella. That would totally throw me off balance. Can we stay with our discussion, please?"

"Most certainly Mirabel. We shall begin with your muddled thoughts. But first let's play with your aura. It's a bit droopy!"

"What do you mean by 'droopy'?"

"Just what we said—droopy. It needs a shot of whiskey or something to get it up and running again."

"Honestly, Bella, you are too much. May we continue with our crazy dialogue?"

"Now, now, it may appear crazy to you, Mirabel, but we are serious little beings at the moment. We don't like to see our favorite earth friend being despondent. So, we shall continue."

"Please do."

"Well, as we were saying, going down 'roads less traveled.' Do you like that, Mirabel? That is one of the great philosophic sayings."

"Yes, I know it, but what has that got to do with me?"

"Well, you are doing just that. It's your nature to take the road less traveled. You love adventure, but when you become stuck in the mud and no one is around to help you out, that's when sparks begin to fly!"

"Well, since you brought it up, Bella, how are you going to help me?"

"Mirabel, ask yourself these questions: What will be the consequence of this? How will it enliven you? Will it be worth all of the effort you put into it? Who will be part of this adventure? How do you go about implementing it? Do you talk it over with a trusted friend? Last but not least, what rewards will it bring you?"

"Bella, it's in the details that I get lost. I either do too much or not enough. That's where the muddiness comes in."

"Yes, you do get befuddled with the details. May I be presumptuous and suggest that you write everything down? Then your mind will relax."

"Already I'm becoming relaxed. My inner wisdom, that quiet voice was telling me to write it all down last week on one of my escapades into the unknown. I ignored it. Sometimes I just don't want to take a few minutes to do that, and I pay for it. ... What are you doing with my aura now? It looks like long coils of gold. ... What's this?"

"Yes, they are long gold coils. We are straightening out your beautiful aura, Mirabel."

"Yes, but now it has sprung back into giant golden ringlets!"
"Just being whimsical, Mirabel. We think you look gorgeous."

"Bella, I get the point. I'll remember it. How could I forget?"

"Cool it. We are ready to unwind your ringlets. Just relax, oh golden one.... There, now. How do you feel?"

"Heavenly! Actually, I feel soft and calm. Thank you, Bella. I'm ready for the day."

"Good. We are off to play, but we'll check in on you from time to time. We'll tweak you if we see you are getting stuck or too engrossed. Just think how gross you would be if you were engrossed!"

"Bella don't go there. I'm saying good-bye. I will be back, I promise. Au revoir."

"Don't worry, we will hold you to your promise! Au revoir, Mirabel. Until we meet again. Remember that song?"

Message: When you jump into activities without forethought and without checking in with your heart, things can get messy. When this happens, writing everything down can take you out of your head and allow you to relax.

Gates

"Good morning, Bella! What's going on? And what are you doing with those gates? Your pals are carrying gates, too. In fact, some of them are puffing because the gates are so heavy."

"Good morning, Mirabel. We have a gargantuan task this morning."

"Oh, really, and are the gates part of this 'gargantuan task'?"

"I detect a note of sarcasm in your voice, Mirabel. It's not becoming to you."

"Oh, don't get huffy with me. I'm just wondering what I'm in for this morning."

"Well, now, since you asked—we are in for a gate ride! All of these gates represent the journeys you have taken on your spiritual path, Mirabel. Each gate represents an opening to a new journey."

"This should prove interesting. I notice all of the gates have different designs. Is there any reason for this?"

"No, we are just making it interesting. And, yes, in a way they do have significance."

"Mmm, you have me thinking."

"Ah, we don't want you to think, Mirabel. You have been doing too much of that again."

"So, you noticed. Is that why you're on my back?" "No, we just want to stir up your brain cells!"

"Funny, let's get on with it. I can't imagine what use the gates have."

"Wait and see. Now, where shall we begin? I must blow myself up into a professor for this task."

"Bella, quit it. We're getting away from the subject, and you look ridiculous. Your beard is too long."

"I know, I know, Mirabel. I am trying your patience this morning."

"Well, if you're going to continue to use delaying tactics, I will shoot you away. Can we get on with it?"

"Yes, gentle soul, we will get on with it. Mirabel, you are on another grand journey, and we have been trying to get your attention. You are so immersed in it that you have forgotten to step back. You want to get it over with. You know from past experience, Mirabel, this doesn't work."

"Yes, you are right Bella, but I don't see how gates have anything to do with it."

"Gates, Mirabel, have everything to do with it. How many gates have you opened and shut on your journey here, Mirabel? I am talking about physical gates."

"Probably once a month. We don't have too many gates around here."

"That is true, Mirabel, but what is the significance of opening a gate?"

"To enter in, to go beyond or go somewhere, I guess."

"Yes, Mirabel, 'to enter in.' we will use that phrase for our purposes here. All of your unfolding journeys, Mirabel, have gates in front of them. You decide as you approach a gate whether you will walk the path behind that gate. The gates are symbolic. They represent all the journeys you will take. Some gates will remain closed, others will open for you, and others will not be opened until you return to your spiritual home."

"Bella, I see a whole field of gates stretching out in various directions. And some are golden, some black, and some opaque, and some are rusty, and they all have different patterns. It's neat."

"Indeed, it is, Mirabel. Let us go to the rusty gate. You tried to open this last week, but it resisted your tugging, and you were swearing. We were there chuckling at your efforts."

"Thanks, Bella. What's happened to your compassion?"

"Now, Mirabel, you are still peeved about this gate. You got it open eventually, but then you hesitated on the threshold, because all you saw was a rutted path with tangled briars on either side of it, some of them stretching across the path. And you decided it was too messy to walk. So, you stood at the gate and then endeavored to close it. 'Another time,' you thought. But it wouldn't close, and you are now faced with walking this path, no stepping back from it. You can hang around the gate for as long as you want to, but eventually you have to make a decision. Its decision time Mirabel!"

"Bella STOP. What are you doing waving a big stick at me? What are you trying to tell me?"

"It's not me, Mirabel, it's you! You opened a gate that was the entrance to one of your buried treasures!"

"Treasures? Would you please explain?"

"Of course, oh, golden one. You didn't know you had a wealth of treasure stored behind this gate, did you?"

"No Bella. This had better be good."

"Yes, Mirabel, you are about to uncover your greatest treasure."

"Phew, I wonder about that. Look at all of those briars and that rutted path."

"Yes, that is part of your journey, Mirabel. And we will be there with you, bringing a sense of humor to you—that is, if you choose to have a sense of humor!"

"Oh, Bella, what am I in for?"

"Relax, golden one. We will help you."

"Now there are dozens of you, Bella, all armed with hatchets, spades and pick axes. And the spade you are carrying is bigger than you. Let's stay with the subject, shall we."

"Really, Mirabel, you are impatient. Don't you see that all you have to do is ask us when you need a bit of digging and clearing done on your journeys?"

"Yes, but what is all this stuff?"

"Ah, Mirabel, it's all of your dusty, messy unfinished projects. Look at this one—it's all tangled, just like the briars. We will begin untangling this one first. ... Okay, helpers, bring in the machetes and hatchets. It's time for a clear-up so that Mirabel can uncover a treasure!"

"Yippee!"

"This is fun! We all get to use our new tools!"

"Okay, Mirabel, are you ready?"

"Ye gods, Bella, what have you brought in—an army of elves?"

"Watch, Mirabel. They will do the heavy clearing for you. You see, oh golden one, you have earned this cleanup crew. In the past you have gone through many gates and walked your journeys in fearlessness and trust. This rusty gate will now be oiled and painted so that you can walk the journey behind it with mastery and pride. The rutted path will be smoothed out for you and the briars cut back. They will blossom before you, giving off their perfume to delight you as you walk this journey into sunlight."

"Oh, Bella, I feel like crying. It's beautiful. I see butterflies, dragonflies, bees, and the briars are blossoming. And I can smell their sweet perfume. You have given me much this day, Bella."

"No, Mirabel, you have gifted yourself. We are merely uncovering the treasures you have earned. This journey you walked is your release from the past—all that stuff buried in your deep, deep self, just waiting to be freed up so that it could see the sunlight and revel in its warmth. Just hanging out with the bees, the blossoms, was all it desired. That old box of memories is cleaned out. Its contents are stretching their wings and rejoicing at their release. They can now fly back to their places of origin. Allow them to go, Mirabel. They were your toys of the past, but now that you are grown, they are of no use to you anymore."

"Well, Bella, you have certainly taken my breath away this time! I don't know what to say."

"Don't say anything, Mirabel, we will do the saying."

"Now, Bella, what are you up to? SINGING! Oh, no! Stop! Your chorus is deafening. And you are all out of tune. Bella. My ears can't take it!"

"Ha-ha, Mirabel. Yes, we are off key, but we are singing and stomping in delight for you. Good-bye golden one."

"Yes, you are right, Bella. Be off with you. Let me digest this beautiful lesson."

Message: The gates are openings to new journeys that you walk while on your spiritual path. They are symbolic. Some gates open to uncomfortable journeys, and it's through these that you discover your greatest treasures.

Endnotes

1. The etheric body, a field of light, is the matrix "blueprint" for the physical body.